OCCASIONAL PAPER 203

Modern Banking and OTC Derivatives Markets

The Transformation of Global Finance and its Implications for Systemic Risk

Garry J. Schinasi, R. Sean Craig,
Burkhard Drees, and Charles Kramer

INTERNATIONAL MONETARY FUND
Washington DC
2000

© 2000 International Monetary Fund

Production: IMF Graphics Section
Figures: Choon Lee
Typesetting: Alicia Etchebarne-Bourdin

Library of Congress Cataloging-in-Publication Data

Schinasi, Garry J.
   Modern banking and OTC derivatives markets: the transformation of global
finance and its implications for systemic risk/Garry J. Schinasi . . . [et al.].

   p. cm.—(Occasional paper/International Monetary Fund; 203)
   Includes bibliographical references.
   ISBN 1-55775-999-5

   1. Derivative securities. 2. Over-the-counter markets. 3. International finance. 4. Risk. I. Title. II. Occasional paper (International Monetary Fund);
no. 203.

HG6024.A3 S355 2000

332.63'2—dc21   00-066083

Price: US$20.00
(US$17.50 to full-time faculty members and
students at universities and colleges)

Please send orders to:
International Monetary Fund, Publication Services
700 19th Street, N.W., Washington, D.C. 20431, U.S.A.
Tel.: (202) 623-7430   Telefax: (202) 623-7201
E-mail: publications@imf.org
Internet: http://www.imf.org

recycled paper

Contents

The following symbols have been used throughout this paper:

. . . to indicate that data are not available;

—   to indicate that the figure is zero or less than half the final digit shown, or that the item does not exist;

–   between years or months (e.g., 1998–99 or January–June) to indicate the years or months covered, including the beginning and ending years or months;

/   between years (e.g., 1998/99) to indicate a fiscal (financial) year.

"Billion" means a thousand million.

Minor discrepancies between constituent figures and totals are due to rounding.

The term "country," as used in this paper, does not in all cases refer to a territorial entity that is a state as understood by international law and practice; the term also covers some territorial entities that are not states, but for which statistical data are maintained and provided internationally on a separate and independent basis.

Preface

This Occasional Paper describes and analyzes key elements of modern banking and the global OTC derivatives markets that are relevant to a consideration of systemic financial risk in the international financial system. While acknowledging and taking as given the considerable benefits that derivatives have conveyed to global finance and international financial markets, the paper identifies and examines sources of risk to market stability, and imperfections in the underlying institutional and market infrastructures. Because relatively limited progress has been made in addressing some of the problems that surfaced during the near-collapse of the hedge fund Long-Term Capital Management (in the autumn of 1998) and the market turbulence that followed, several areas are identified where further efforts are necessary if the risks of financial instability are to be reduced and avoided, and if the efficiency gains of modern finance are to be preserved.

This paper is the product of a team effort led by Garry J. Schinasi, Chief of the Capital Markets and Financial Studies Division in the IMF's Research Department. The team of authors, which also included R. Sean Craig, Burkhard Drees, and Charles Kramer, benefited from a series of discussions with officials and market participants in Frankfurt, London, New York, Paris, and Tokyo during 1999 and 2000. The authors are grateful for comments by Michael Mussa (Economic Counsellor and Director of Research), R. Todd Smith, and other colleagues in the IMF. Subramanian Sriram and Oksana Khadarina provided research assistance, Caroline Bagworth and Adriana Vohden prepared the manuscript, and Jeremy Clift of the External Relations Department coordinated its publication. The paper draws on material published in previous issues of the IMF's annual *International Capital Markets* report, and some of the project's findings are published as Chapter IV of *International Capital Markets: Developments, Prospects, and Key Policy Issues* (September 2000). The views expressed in this Occasional Paper are those of the participating IMF staff and do not necessarily reflect the views of market participants, national authorities, or the IMF.

I   Overview

The rapid growth, development, and widespread use of over-the-counter (OTC) derivatives have accompanied, and in many ways made possible, the modernization of commercial and investment banking and the globalization of finance. OTC derivatives instruments and markets have developed rapidly along with the emergence and evolution of the internationally active financial institutions that presently intermediate the bulk of international capital flows and capital in the major financial markets around the globe. These and other financial structural changes would not have been possible without the dramatic advances in information and computer technologies that have occurred during the past two decades.

Because of their flexibility, OTC derivatives bestow considerable benefits by allowing financial risks to be more precisely tailored to risk preferences and tolerances. They have contributed to the development of a more complete (and efficient) set of financial markets, improved market liquidity, depth, and breadth, and increased the capacity of the financial system to bear and price risk and allocate capital. As a result, OTC derivatives instruments, the structures for trading and risk-managing them, and the infrastructures for ensuring their smooth functioning play a central role in the performance of the major financial and capital markets. Overall, OTC derivatives activities have contributed significantly to the effectiveness and efficiency of the international financial system.

Along with these fundamental positive contributions, as crises in the 1990s have demonstrated, OTC derivatives activities can contribute to the buildup of vulnerabilities and adverse market dynamics in some circumstances. The severity of turbulence in the 1990s, and in particular the contours of the market dynamics in the aftermath of the near-collapse of the hedge fund Long-Term Capital Management (LTCM) in the autumn of 1998, suggest that OTC derivatives activities are capable of producing instability, in some cases akin to a modern form of traditional bank runs. The virulence of the 1998 turbulence in the mature financial markets took market participants and authorities by surprise, and some

authorities have acknowledged that they do not fully understand the rapidly changing structure and dynamics of global financial markets. A substantial buildup in derivatives credit exposures and leverage contributed importantly to the turbulence. This substantial leverage—LTCM accumulated $1.2 trillion in notional positions on equity of $5 billion—was possible primarily because of the existence of large, liquid OTC derivatives markets.

In the wake of episodes of financial turbulence during the 1990s, much has been written about derivatives instruments and the role of highly leveraged institutions in international financial markets.[1] By contrast, little has been written about how the increased reliance on OTC derivatives activities and *market structures* by the systemically important, internationally active financial institutions may have changed the nature of systemic risks in the international financial system. This paper attempts to fill part of this analytical gap, in part by building upon a broad overview of market practices, market structure, and official supervision and regulation in financial markets. Rather than exhaustively examine all details in these areas, this Occasional Paper highlights the key features of modern banking and OTC derivatives markets that seem to be relevant for assessing their functioning, their implications for systemic financial risks in the international financial system, and areas where improvements in ensuring financial stability can be obtained.

The layout of the paper is as follows. In Section II, the paper describes how OTC derivatives activities have transformed modern financial intermediation. It discusses how internationally active financial institutions have become exposed to additional sources of instability because of their large and dynamic exposures to the counterparty (credit) risks embodied in their OTC derivatives activities. Section III outlines the structure of the OTC derivatives markets in its present-day form, describes some of the key elements of market practice, including trading and risk management, and highlights the key

---

[1]See International Monetary Fund (1999), Chapter IV.

differences between organized-exchange and OTC markets. Section IV provides an overview of the regulatory environment for OTC derivatives activities and markets in key jurisdictions, with particular emphasis on how regulations affect the location and legal entities for OTC derivatives transactions and how regulatory uncertainties can affect OTC derivatives activities. Section V summarizes and distills the key features of OTC derivatives markets that have potential implications for systemic risk, and thereby provides analytical perspective on their functioning. Section VI concentrates on financial stability issues and identifies sources of risk to market stability and imperfections in the underlying infrastructure. Progress in addressing some of these risks and imperfections has been limited, and the next section identifies areas where further efforts are necessary if the risks of instability are to be reduced and avoided in the future. Section VIII summarizes the main conclusions of the paper. An Appendix reviews the historical roots of the OTC derivatives markets.

II Modern Banking and OTC Derivatives Markets

During the past two decades, the large internationally active financial institutions have transformed the business of finance dramatically. In doing so, they have improved the ability to manage, price, trade, and intermediate capital worldwide. Many of these benefits have come from the development, broadening, and deepening of, and greater reliance on, OTC derivatives activities (see Box 2.1: Precision Finance, Desegmentation and Conglomeration, and Market Integration). Although modern financial institutions still derive most of their earnings from intermediating, pricing, and managing credit risk, they are doing increasingly more of it off balance sheet, and in less transparent and potentially riskier ways. This transformation has accelerated during the 1990s.

The Transformation of Global Finance

Traditional banking involves extending loans on borrowed funds (deposits) of different maturities. Each side of this ledger has different financial risks. A simple loan is for a fixed sum, term, and interest rate; in return the bank is promised a known schedule of fixed payments. The risk in lending, of course, is that the borrower may become unable or unwilling to make each fixed payment on schedule. This is credit (or counterparty) risk,[2] comprising both the risk of default (missing one or all payments) and the expected loss given default (that less than is promised is paid). Loans are funded by deposits with much shorter maturities than most bank loans, which imparts liquidity risk. The basic business of banking is to manage these two sets of cash flows, each having a different, stochastic structure. As the history of bank runs and failures indicates, managing these cashflows is inherently risky and banking is prone to instability.[3]

This tendency toward instability does not seem to have diminished in the 1990s, and may have increased. In modern finance, financial institutions'

off-balance-sheet business entails extensions of credit. For example, a simple swap transaction is a two-way credit instrument in which each counterparty promises to make a schedule of payments over the life of the contract. Each counterparty is both a creditor and debtor and, as in traditional banking, the modern financial institution has to manage the cash inflows (the creditor position) and outflows (the debtor position) associated with the derivatives contract. But there are important differences. First, the embedded credit risk is considerably more complicated and less predictable than the credit risk in a simple loan because the credit exposures associated with derivatives are time-varying and depend on the prices of underlying assets. Traditional bank lending is largely insulated from market risk because banks carry loans on the balance sheet at book value, meaning they may not recognize and need not respond to market shocks. Nevertheless, market developments can contribute to unrecognized losses that can accumulate over time. By contrast, OTC credit exposures are subject to volatile market risk and are, as a matter of course, marked to market every day. This creates highly variable profit-and-loss performance, but it imparts market discipline and also avoids undetected accumulations of losses. Day-to-day shifts in the constellation of asset prices can have a considerable impact on credit risk exposures—both the exposures borne by any particular financial institution and the distribution and concentration of such exposures throughout the international financial system.

Second, the dynamics of modern finance are considerably more complex than those of deposit markets. Deposit flows have a degree of regularity associated with the flow of underlying business. By contrast, flows associated with OTC derivatives and liquidity conditions in these markets, and in related markets, can be highly irregular and difficult to predict, even for the most technically advanced dealers with state-of-the-art risk management systems. Overall, the stochastic processes that govern the cash flows associated with OTC derivatives are inherently more difficult to understand, and seem to be more unstable during periods of extreme volatility in underlying asset prices.

---

[2]See the Glossary for definitions of special terms.
[3]See Bryant (1980), Diamond and Dybvig (1983), and Kindleberger (1989).

Box 2.1. Precision Finance, Desegmentation and Conglomeration, and Market Integration[1]

The main changes that have characterized the globalization of finance and risk can be summarized in the following points:

- Greater use of modern precision finance to unbundle, price, trade, and manage complex financial risks.
- Transformation of banking from concentration on lending (leverage and maturity transformation are traditional definitions of banks), to diversification into fee- and service-based businesses.
- Transformation of balance-sheet activities into securitized loans and off-balance-sheet positions.
- Rapid and continued growth in the importance of institutional investors, and the associated bank disintermediation; institutional investors manage more than $23 trillion.

- Conglomeration of financial activities into large institutions providing traditional banking, investment banking, insurance, and other financial services.
- Emergence of internationally active (global) financial institutions (banks, institutional investors, and conglomerates).
- More highly integrated markets, with greater diversity in the quality, sophistication, and geographic origins of borrowers and lenders.
- Larger exposures to non-home markets.

The confluence of these changes has been associated with: greater mobility of capital; an accelerated expansion of cross-border financial activity; greater interdependencies between market participants, markets, and financial systems; greater market efficiency and liquidity in international markets; and faster speeds of adjustment of financial flows and asset prices.

---

[1]See Annex V in International Monetary Fund (1998).

Table 2.1. Top Twenty Derivatives Dealers in 2000 and Their Corresponding Ranks in 1999

Derivatives Dealers	Rank 2000	Rank 1999	CME	LIFFE	EUREX	HKFE	TSE	TIFFE
Citigroup	1	1	x	x	x	x	x	
Goldman, Sachs & Co.	2	2	x	x	x	x	x	
Deutsche Bank[1]	3	6	x	x	x	x	x	
Morgan Stanley Dean Witter	4	4	x	x	x	x	x	
Warburg Dillon Read	5	7	x	x	x	x	x	
Merrill Lynch & Co.	6	5	x	x	x	x	x	
J.P. Morgan	7	3	x	x	x	x	x	
Chase Manhattan Corp.	8	8	x	x	x			x
Credit Suisse First Boston	9	9	x	x	x	x	x	
Bank of America	10	11	x	x	x			x
NatWest Group	11	n.a.		x	x			x
Lehman Brothers	12	12	x	x	x	x	x	
Hong Kong and Shanghai Banking Corp.	13	16	x	x	x	x	x	x
Société Générale	14	13	x	x	x			
American International Group	15	19	x					
Barclays Capital	16	14	x	x	x	x	x	x
Dresdner Kleinwort Benson	17	n.a.	x	x	x	x		
BNP-Paribas[2]	18	18	x	x	x	x	x	
ABN Amro	19	17	x	x	x	x	x	
Commerzbank	20	n.a.	x	x	x	x		

Source: Clow (2000), pp. 121–25.

[1]Includes BT Alex. Brown for 2000.

[2]Ranking of Banque Paribas for 1999.

[3]Chicago Mercantile Exchange (CME); London International Financial Futures and Options Exchange (LIFFE); European Derivatives Market (EUREX); Hong Kong Futures Exchange (HKFE); Tokyo Stock Exchange (TSE); and Tokyo International Financial Futures Exchange (TIFFE).

Thus, in addition to assessing and managing the risk of default and the expected loss given default, the modern financial institution has to assess the potential change in the value of the credit extended and form expectations about the future path of underlying asset prices. This, in turn, requires an under-

---

Box 2.2. The Role of OTC Currency Options in the Dollar-Yen Market

OTC derivatives activities can exacerbate disturbances in underlying markets—even some of the largest markets, such as foreign exchange markets. This was, for example, the case in the dollar-yen market in March 1995 and October 1998; once the yen had appreciated beyond a certain level, the cancellation of OTC knockout options and the unwinding of associated hedging positions fueled the momentum toward further appreciation.[1] During these periods of heightened exchange rate volatility, OTC derivatives activities also significantly influenced exchange-traded option markets, because standard exchange-traded options were used by derivatives dealers as hedging vehicles for OTC currency options.

In 1995, the yen appreciated vis-à-vis the dollar from ¥101 in early January to ¥80 in mid-April, strengthening by 7 percent in four trading sessions between March 2 and March 7. A combination of macroeconomic factors was widely cited as having contributed to the initial exchange rate move. The speed of the move also suggests that technical factors (such as the cancellation of knockout options) and short-term trading conditions (such as the unwinding of yen-carry trades, also involving OTC derivatives) reinforced the trend. In early 1995, relatively large volumes of down-and-out dollar put options were purchased by Japanese exporters to partially hedge the yen value of dollar receivables against a moderate yen appreciation.

In September–October 1998, the yen again appreciated sharply vis-à-vis the dollar from ¥135 to ¥120 per dollar. Of particular interest are the developments during October 6–9, 1998, when the yen strengthened by 15 percent in relation to the dollar. Talk of an additional fiscal stimulus package in Japan and a reassessment of the relative monetary policy stances in Japan and the United States may have sparked the initial rally in the yen and corresponding weakening in the dollar. The initial spate of dollar selling, in turn, was viewed as having created the sentiment that the dollar's long-standing strengthening vis-à-vis the yen had run its course. But, as in March 1995, in addition to reversals of yen-carry trades, knockout options were widely viewed as having provided additional momentum that boosted demand for yen and contributed to the dollar selling.

Knockout options (a type of OTC barrier option) differ from standard options in that they are canceled if the exchange rate reaches certain knockout levels, and therefore leave the investor unhedged against large exchange rate movements. Nonetheless, they are widely used since they are less expensive than standard options. In 1995 and 1998, knockout options, particularly down-and-out put options on the dollar, amplified exchange rate dynamics through two separate channels: (1) Japanese exporters who bought knockout options to protect against a moderate depreciation of the dollar sold dollars into a declining market when the knockout options were canceled to prevent further losses on their dollar receivables; and (2) dynamic hedging strategies employed by sellers of knockout options required the sudden sale of dollars after the knockout levels had been reached (see Box 3.3). Ironically, OTC knockout options that protect only against moderate exchange rate fluctuations can sometimes increase the likelihood of large exchange rate movements—the very event they do not protect against.

Although knockout options represented a relatively small share of total outstanding currency options (between 2 and 12 percent), they had a profound effect on the market for standard exchange-traded options. It is easy to see why: knockout options are sometimes hedged by a portfolio of standard options. Dealers who employed this hedging technique needed to buy a huge amount of standard options at the same time as other market participants were trying to contain losses from canceled down-and-out puts. As a consequence, prices of exchange-traded put options (implied volatilities) doubled in March 1995 and almost doubled in October 1998.

---

[1]See International Monetary Fund (1996, and 1998b, Box 3.1) and Malz (1995).

---

standing of the underlying asset markets and establishes a link between derivatives and underlying asset markets.

Importance of OTC Derivatives in Modern Banking and Global Finance

The unpredictable, and at times turbulent, nature of OTC derivatives markets would merit little concern if OTC derivatives were an insignificant part of the world of global finance. They are not, and they are increasingly central to global finance. OTC derivatives markets are large, at mid-2000 comprising $94 trillion in notional principal, the reference amount for payments, and $2.6 trillion in (off-balance-sheet) credit exposures (see Section III). The markets comprise the major international financial institutions (Table 2.1), and together the instruments and markets interlink the array of global financial markets through a variety of channels.[4]

In the past two decades, the major internationally active financial institutions have significantly increased the share of their earnings from derivatives activities, including from trading fees and propri-

---

[4]See the discussion of spillovers and contagion in International Monetary Fund (1998a).

Box 2.3. LTCM and Turbulence in Global Financial Markets[1]

The turbulent dynamics in global capital markets in late 1998 had been preceded by a steady buildup of positions and prices in the mature equity and bond markets during the years and months preceding the Russian crisis in mid-August 1998 and the near collapse of the hedge fund LTCM in September. The bullish conditions in the major financial markets continued through the early summer of 1998, amid earlier warning signs that many advanced country equity markets, not just in the United States, were reaching record and perhaps unsustainable levels. As early as mid–1997, differences in the cost of borrowing between high- and low-risk borrowers began to narrow to the point where several advanced country central banks sounded warnings that credit spreads were reaching relatively low levels and that lending standards had been relaxed in some countries beyond a reasonable level. A complex network of derivatives counterparty exposures, encompassing a very high degree of leverage, had accumulated in the major markets through late summer 1998. The credit exposures and high degree of leverage both reflected the relatively low margin requirements on over-the-counter derivative transactions and the increasingly accepted practice of very low, or zero, "haircuts" on repo transactions.

Although the weakening of credit standards and complacency with overall risk management had benefited a large number of market participants, including a variety of highly leveraged institutions (HLIs), LTCM's reputation for having the best technicians as well as its high profitability during its relatively brief history earned it a particularly highly valued counterparty status. Many of the major internationally active financial institutions actively courted LTCM, seeking to be LTCM's creditor, trader, and counterparty. By August 1998, and with less than $5 billion of equity capi-

tal, LTCM had assembled a trading book that involved nearly 60,000 trades, including on-balance-sheet positions totaling $125 billion and off-balance-sheet positions that included nearly $1 trillion of notional OTC derivative positions and more than $500 billion of notional exchange-traded derivatives positions. These very large and highly leveraged trading positions spanned most of the major fixed income, securities, and foreign exchange markets, and involved as counterparties many of the financial institutions at the core of global financial markets.

Sentiment weakened generally throughout the summer of 1998 and deteriorated sharply in August when the devaluation and unilateral debt restructuring by Russia sparked a period of turmoil in mature markets that was virtually without precedent in the absence of a major inflationary or economic shock. The crisis in Russia sparked a broad-based reassessment and repricing of risk and large-scale deleveraging and portfolio rebalancing that cut across a range of global financial markets. In September and early October, indications of heightened concern about liquidity and counterparty risk emerged in some of the world's deepest financial markets.

A key development was the news of difficulties in, and ultimately the near-failure of, LTCM, an important market-maker and provider of liquidity in securities markets. LTCM's size and high leverage made it particularly exposed to the adverse shift in market sentiment following the Russian event. On July 31, 1998, LTCM had $4.1 billion in capital, down from just under $5 billion at the start of the year. During August alone, LTCM lost an additional $1.8 billion, and LTCM approached investors for an injection of capital.

In early September 1998, the possible default and/or bankruptcy of LTCM was a major concern in financial markets. Market reverberations intensified as major market participants scrambled to shed risk with LTCM and other counterparties, including in the commercial paper market, and to increase the liquidity of their posi-

---

[1]This box draws on the analysis in International Monetary Fund (1998b, 1999).

etary trading profits. These institutions manage portfolios of derivatives involving tens of thousand of positions, and daily aggregate global turnover now stands at roughly $1 trillion. The market can be seen as an informal network of bilateral counterparty relationships and dynamic, time-varying credit exposures whose size and distribution are intimately tied to important asset markets. Because each derivatives portfolio is composed of positions in a wide variety of markets, the network of credit exposures is inherently complex and difficult to manage. During periods in which financial market conditions stay within historical norms, credit exposures exhibit a predictable level of volatility, and risk management systems can, within a tolerable

range of uncertainty, assess the riskiness of exposures. Risk management systems guide the rebalancing of the large OTC derivatives portfolios, which in normal periods can enhance the efficient allocation of risks among firms, but which can also be a source of trading and price variability—especially in times of financial stress—that feeds back into the stochastic nature of the cashflows.

Expansions and contractions in the level of OTC derivatives activities are a normal part of modern finance and typically occur in a nondisruptive manner, if not smoothly, even when there is isolated turbulence in one underlying market. The potential for excessively rapid contractions and instability seems to emerge when credit exposures in OTC actions. LTCM's previous "preferred creditor" status evaporated, its credit lines were withdrawn, and margin calls on the fund accelerated. The major concerns were the consequences—for asset prices and for the health of LTCM's main counterparties—of having to unwind LTCM's very large positions as well as how much longer LTCM would be able to meet mounting daily margin calls. As a result, LTCM's main counterparties demanded additional collateral. On September 21, Bear Stearns—LTCM's prime brokerage firm—required LTCM to put up additional collateral to cover potential settlement exposures. Default by as early as September 23 was perceived as a very real possibility for LTCM in the absence of an injection of capital.

In response to these developments and the rapid deleveraging, market volatility increased sharply, and there were some significant departures from normal pricing relationships among different asset classes. In the U.S. treasury market, for example, the spread between the yields of "on-the-run" and "off-the-run" treasuries widened from less than 10 basis points to about 15 basis points in the wake of the Russian debt restructuring, and to a peak of over 35 basis points in mid-October, suggesting that investors were placing an unusually large premium on the liquidity of the "on-the-run" issue. Spreads between yields in the eurodollar market and on U.S. treasury bills for similar maturities also widened to historically high levels, as did spreads between commercial paper and treasury bills and those between the fixed leg of fixed-for-floating interest rate swaps and government bond yields, pointing to heightened concerns about counterparty risk. Interest rate swap spreads widened in currencies including the U.S. dollar, deutsche mark, and pound sterling. In the U.K. money markets, the spread of sterling interbank rates over general collateral repo rates rose sharply during the fourth quarter, partly owing to concerns about liquidity and counterparty risk (and also reflecting a desire for end-of-year liquidity).

As securities prices fell, market participants with leveraged securities positions sold those and other se-

curities to meet margin calls, adding to the decline in prices. The decline in prices and rise in market volatility also led arbitrageurs and market-makers in the securities markets to cut positions and inventories and withdraw from market-making, reducing liquidity in securities markets and exacerbating the decline in prices. In this environment, considerable uncertainty about how much an unwinding of positions by LTCM and similar institutions might contribute to selling pressure fed concerns that the cycle of price declines and deleveraging might accelerate.

In response to these developments, central banks in major advanced economies cut official interest rates. In the United States, an initial cut on September 29 failed to significantly calm markets; spreads continued to widen, equity markets fell further, and volatility continued to increase. Against this background, the Federal Reserve followed up on October 15 with a cut in both the federal funds target and the discount rate, a key policy action that stemmed and ultimately helped reverse the deteriorating trend in market sentiment. The easing—coming so soon after the first rate cut and outside a regular FOMC meeting (the first such move since April 1994)—sent a clear signal that the U.S. monetary authorities were prepared to move aggressively if needed to ensure the normal functioning of financial markets.

Calm began to return to money and credit markets in mid-October. Money market spreads declined quickly to precrisis levels, while credit spreads declined more slowly and remained somewhat above precrisis levels, probably reflecting the deleveraging. The Federal Reserve cut both the federal funds target and the discount rate at the FOMC meeting on November 17, noting that although financial market conditions had settled down materially since mid-October, unusual strains remained. Short-term spreads subsequently declined. The calming effect of the rate cuts suggested that the turbulence stemmed primarily from a sudden and sharp increase in pressures on (broadly defined) liquidity, including securities market liquidity, triggered by a reassessment of risk.

tivities rise to levels that create hypersensitivity to sudden unanticipated changes in market conditions (such as interest rate spreads) and new information. The creditor and debtor relationships implicit in OTC derivatives transactions between the internationally active financial institutions can create situations in which the possibility of isolated defaults can threaten the access to liquidity of key market participants—similar to a traditional bank run. This can significantly alter perceptions of market conditions, and particularly perceptions of the riskiness and potential size of OTC derivatives credit exposures. The rapid unwinding of positions, as all counterparties run for liquidity, is characterized by creditors demanding payment, selling collateral,

and putting on hedges, while debtors draw down capital and liquidate other assets. Until OTC derivatives exposures contract to a sustainable level, markets can remain distressed and give rise to systemic problems. This is what happened in 1998: after it became known that LTCM might default, some dealers were concerned that their dealer counterparties were heavily exposed to LTCM. The induced changes in market conditions quickly created a run for liquidity.

Greater asset price volatility related to the rebalancing of portfolios may be a reasonable price to pay for the efficiency gains from global finance. However, in the 1990s, OTC derivatives activities have sometimes exhibited an unusual volatility and have added to the historical experience of what volatility can mean. For example, in the 1990s, there were repeated periods of volatility and stress in different asset markets (ERM crises; bond market turbulence in 1994 and 1996; Mexican, Asian, and Russian crises; LTCM; Brazil) as market participants searched for higher rates of return in the world's major bond, equity, foreign exchange, and derivatives markets. Some of these episodes suggest that the structure of market dynamics has been adversely affected by financial innovations and become more unpredictable, if not unstable.

Examples of extreme market volatility include movements in the yen-dollar rate in both 1995 and 1998. In both cases the yen-dollar exchange rate exhibited what might be characterized as extreme price dynamics—beyond what changes in fundamentals would suggest was appropriate—in what was, and is, one of the deepest and most liquid markets. The extreme nature of the price dynamics resulted in part from hedging positions involving the use of OTC derivatives contracts called knockout options (see Box 2.2: The Role of OTC Currency Options in the Dollar-Yen Market, page 5). These OTC options are designed to insure against relatively small changes in an underlying asset price. Yet once a certain threshold level of the yen-dollar rate was reached, the bunching of these OTC options drove the yen-dollar rate to extraordinary levels in a very short period of time—an event that the OTC options were not designed to insure against.

Such episodes of rapid and severe dynamics can also pose risks to systemic stability. In particular, the turbulence surrounding the near-collapse of LTCM in the autumn of 1998 posed the risk of systemic consequences for the international financial system, and seemed to have created consequences for real economic activity (see Box 2.3: LTCM and Turbulence in Global Financial Markets, page 6). This risk was real enough that major central banks reduced interest rates to restore risk taking to a level supportive of more normal levels of financial intermediation and continued economic growth. LTCM's trading books were so complicated and its positions so large that the world's top derivatives traders and risk managers from three major derivatives houses could not determine how to unwind LTCM's derivatives books rapidly in an orderly fashion without retaining LTCM staff to assist in liquidating the large and complex portfolio of positions.

Both private market participants and those responsible for banking supervision and official market surveillance are learning to adapt to the fast pace of innovation and structural change. This challenging learning process has been made more difficult because OTC derivatives activities may have changed the nature of systemic risk in ways that are not yet fully understood.[5] The heavy reliance on OTC derivatives appears to have created the possibility of systemic financial events that fall outside of the more formal clearinghouse structures and official real-time gross-payment settlement systems that are designed to contain and prevent such problems. There is the concern that heavy reliance on new and even more innovative financial techniques, and the possibility that they may create volatile and extreme dynamics, could yet produce even greater turbulence with consequences for real economic activity—perhaps with consequences reaching the proportions of real economic losses typically associated with financial panics and banking crises.

In sum, the internationally active financial institutions have increasingly nurtured the ability to profit from OTC derivatives activities and financial market participants benefit significantly from them. As a result, OTC derivatives activities play a central and predominantly a beneficial role in modern finance. Nevertheless, the important role of OTC derivatives in modern finance, and in particular in recent periods of turbulence, raises the concern that the instabilities associated with modern finance and OTC derivatives markets could give rise to systemic problems that potentially could affect the international financial system.

---

[5]See Greenspan (1998) and Tietmeyer (1999).

III OTC Derivatives Markets: Size, Structure, and Business Practices

This section provides an overview of OTC derivatives markets, with particular emphasis on those aspects that are relevant to an assessment of systemic financial risks. It begins with a description of the size and global scope of derivatives markets and the major participants and counterparties in OTC derivatives markets. It then compares the structures of exchange-traded and OTC markets, and concludes with a discussion of the trading and back-office infrastructure and the middle-office risk management functions for OTC derivatives trading.

The Size, Global Scope, and Institutional Structure of Derivatives Markets

The global derivatives markets are large, both in absolute terms and compared with the size of the global economy and global financial markets (Tables 3.1 and 3.2). At end-June 2000, global notional principal (the reference amount for payments on a derivatives contract) of exchange-traded and OTC derivatives contracts combined totaled about $108 trillion. Turnover in global derivatives markets is similarly large. In 1998, the most recent year for which data on turnover in both OTC and exchange-traded markets is available, estimated average *daily* turnover amounted to about $2.7 trillion (equivalent to $675 trillion on an annualized basis). By comparison, in 1999, world GDP stood at about $31 trillion, and global net capital flows (the sum of all current account surpluses) totaled $394 billion.

OTC derivatives account for an increasing share of the global derivatives markets. During the 1990s, OTC derivatives markets grew from roughly equal to exchange-traded markets in size to several times as large as exchange-traded markets (Figure 3.1). This trend seems to have accelerated in the second half of the 1990s. Between June 1998 and June 2000, global notional principal in OTC derivatives markets rose from $72 trillion to $94 trillion, while notional principal in exchange-

traded markets declined from $14.8 trillion to $13.9 trillion. Between April 1995 and April 1998, average daily turnover in OTC derivatives markets rose by about 50 percent to $1.3 trillion, while turnover on derivatives exchanges rose by only about 16 percent to $1.4 trillion.[6] Because most contracts do not specify the exchange of principal amounts (foreign-exchange and currency swaps—described below—are among the exceptions), gross market value—an estimate of replacement cost, typically around 2 to 5 percent of notional principal—is a better indicator of current credit exposure than notional principal.[7] At end-June 2000, global gross market value of contracts in OTC derivatives markets stood at $2.6 trillion, while credit exposure taking netting arrangements into account stood at about $0.9 trillion (comparable figures for exchange-traded markets are not available).

The bulk of OTC derivatives contracts are associated with interest rate and foreign exchange risks (Figure 3.2). Activity in interest rate derivatives is dominated by swaps, followed by Forward Rate Agreements (FRAs—forwards on interest rates) and options. Turnover in foreign exchange derivatives is dominated by foreign exchange swaps, followed by outright forwards, options, and currency swaps.[8] The comparatively small forward market is oriented toward the retail trading and hedging needs of nonfinancial customers, who account for

---

[6]Turnover data are less timely than data on outstanding amounts.

[7]Gross market value is the sum of the positive market value of all contracts held by the institutions included in the survey, and the negative market value of surveyed institutions' contracts with those not included in the survey. A portfolio of one contract worth $5 and one contract worth –$2 (a negative market value) against a non-reporting institution thus has a gross market value of $7. The overall credit risk in a derivatives portfolio is more complicated to measure, as it includes potential future exposure (see below).

[8]A foreign exchange swap is typically a short-term deal that combines a spot sale of currency and a forward purchase. A currency swap typically has a longer maturity and involves both a spot sale and forward purchase and the periodic exchange of interest in the two currencies.

Table 3.1. Global Over-the-Counter (OTC) Derivatives Markets: Notional Amounts and Gross Market Values of Outstanding Contracts, 1998–2000[1]
(Billions of U.S. dollars)

	Notional Amounts					Gross Market Values				
	End-Jun. 1998	End-Dec. 1998	End-Jun. 1999	End-Dec. 1999	End-Jun. 2000	End-Jun. 1998	End-Dec. 1998	End-Jun. 1999	End-Dec. 1999	End-Jun. 2000
Total	72,143	80,317	81,458	88,201	94,037	2,580	3,231	2,628	2,813	2,581
Foreign exchange	18,719	18,011	14,899	14,344	15,494	799	786	582	662	578
Outright forwards and forex swaps	12,149	12,063	9,541	9,593	10,504	476	491	329	352	283
Currency swaps	1,947	2,253	2,350	2,444	2,605	208	200	192	250	239
Options	4,623	3,695	3,009	2,307	2,385	115	96	61	60	55
Interest rate[2]	42,368	50,015	54,072	60,091	64,125	1,160	1,675	1,357	1,304	1,230
Swaps	29,363	36,262	38,372	43,936	47,993	1,018	1,509	1,222	1,150	1,072
Forward rate agreements	5,147	5,756	7,137	6,775	6,771	33	15	12	12	13
Options	7,858	7,997	8,562	9,380	9,361	108	152	123	141	145
Equity linked	1,274	1,488	1,511	1,809	1,671	190	236	244	359	293
Options	1,120	1,342	1,313	1,527	1,323	170	192	193	288	231
Forwards and swaps	154	146	198	283	348	20	44	52	71	62
Commodity[3]	451	415	441	548	584	38	43	44	59	80
Gold	193	182	189	243	262	10	13	23	23	19
Other	258	233	252	305	323	28	30	22	37	61
Forwards and swaps	153	137	127	163	169	…	…	…	…	…
Options	106	97	125	143	154	…	…	…	…	…
Other[4]	9,331	10,388	10,536	11,408	12,163	393	492	400	429	400

Source: Bank for International Settlements, 2000, "Press Release: The Global OTC Derivatives Market Continues to Grow" (Basel, November 13).

[1]All figures are adjusted for double-counting. Notional amounts outstanding have been adjusted by halving positions vis-à-vis other reporting dealers. Gross market values have been calculated as the sum of the total gross positive market value of contracts and the absolute value of the gross negative market value of contracts with non-reporting counterparties.

[2]Single-currency contracts only.

[3]Adjustments for double-counting are estimated.

[4]For end-June 1998: positions reported by institutions that only participated in the 1998 Triennial Survey of Foreign Exchange and Derivatives Market Activity; for subsequent periods: estimated positions of those institutions.

about a third of turnover.[9] Trading in OTC derivatives is denominated in the main international currencies. Overall, about half of OTC foreign exchange derivatives exposure involves the U.S. dollar; in 2000, in the interest rate segment, euro-denominated exposures were somewhat larger than dollar exposures.

OTC derivatives markets are global in scope. Trading is concentrated in the major financial centers: in 1998, London accounted for 35 percent of daily turnover, while New York accounted for 17 percent and Tokyo 7 percent (Table 3.3). A considerable share of trading—over half of currency swaps and single-currency interest-rate swaps—is cross-border. Much of this activity is accounted for by internationally active banks; for example, foreign-owned firms are major participants in the U.K. OTC derivatives markets.[10] Similarly, in 1998, major U.S. banks earned larger revaluation gains on overseas derivatives activities than on domestic derivatives activities.[11]

As the major internationally active banks and securities houses dominate the OTC derivatives markets, the market is highly concentrated: in the second quarter of 2000, seven U.S. banks held over 95

---

[9]The average deal size of spot and forward transactions in the United States is approximately $4 million, whereas the average notional size of foreign exchange swaps is nearly eight times as large. Long-term transactions (one year and longer to maturity) account for less than 4 percent of traditional foreign currency derivatives turnover.

[10]Thom and Boustani (1998).

[11]See United States, Board of Governors of the Federal Reserve System (1999), Table 5.

Table 3.2. Global Over-the-Counter (OTC) Derivatives Markets: Notional Amounts and Gross Market Values of Outstanding Contracts by Counterparty, Remaining Maturity, and Currency Composition, 1998–2000[1]

(Billions of U.S. dollars)

	Notional Amounts					Gross Market Values				
	End-Jun. 1998	End-Dec. 1998	End-Jun. 1999	End-Dec. 1999	End-Jun. 2000	End-Jun. 1998	End-Dec. 1998	End-Jun. 1999	End-Dec. 1999	End-Jun. 2000
Total	72,143	80,317	81,458	88,201	94,037	2,580	3,231	2,628	2,813	2,581
Foreign exchange	18,719	18,011	14,899	14,344	15,494	799	786	582	662	578
By counterparty										
With other reporting dealers	7,406	7,284	5,464	5,392	5,827	314	336	200	214	168
With other financial institutions	7,048	7,440	6,429	6,102	6,421	299	297	246	281	242
With non-financial customers	4,264	3,288	3,007	2,850	3,246	186	153	136	167	168
By remaining maturity										
Up to one year[2]	16,292	15,791	12,444	12,140	13,178	...	...	...	...	...
One to five years[2]	1,832	1,624	1,772	1,539	1,623	...	...	...	...	...
Over five years[2]	595	592	683	666	693	...	...	...	...	...
By major currency										
U.S. dollar[3]	16,167	15,810	13,181	12,834	13,961	747	698	519	581	518
Euro[3,4]	8,168	7,658	4,998	4,667	5,863	193	223	206	239	242
Japanese yen[3]	5,579	5,319	4,641	4,236	4,344	351	370	171	262	157
Pound sterling[3]	2,391	2,612	2,281	2,242	2,479	55	62	63	55	76
Other[3]	5,133	4,623	4,697	4,709	4,342	252	219	205	187	162
Interest rate[5]	42,368	50,015	54,072	60,091	64,125	1,160	1,675	1,357	1,304	1,230
By counterparty										
With other reporting dealers	18,244	24,442	27,059	30,518	32,208	463	748	634	602	560
With other financial institutions	18,694	19,790	21,149	24,012	25,771	515	683	559	548	518
With non-financial customers	5,430	5,783	5,863	5,562	6,146	182	244	164	154	152
By remaining maturity										
Up to one year[2]	17,422	18,185	20,287	24,874	25,809	...	...	...	...	...
One to five years[2]	16,805	21,405	21,985	23,179	24,406	...	...	...	...	...
Over five years[2]	8,141	10,420	11,800	12,038	13,910	...	...	...	...	...
By major currency										
U.S. dollar	13,214	13,763	16,073	16,510	17,606	311	370	337	376	367
Euro[4]	13,576	16,461	17,483	20,692	22,948	476	786	584	492	467
Japanese yen	7,164	9,763	10,207	12,391	12,763	194	212	192	232	207
Pound sterling	3,288	3,911	4,398	4,588	4,741	59	130	103	94	84
Other	5,126	6,117	5,911	5,910	6,068	120	177	141	110	105
Equity-linked	1,274	1,488	1,511	1,809	1,671	190	236	244	359	293
Commodity[6]	451	415	441	548	584	38	43	44	59	80
Other[7]	9,331	10,388	10,536	11,408	12,163	393	492	400	429	400

Source: Bank for International Settlements, 2000, "Press Release: The Global OTC Derivatives Market Continues to Grow" (Basel, November 13).

[1]All figures are adjusted for double-counting. Notional amounts outstanding have been adjusted by halving positions vis-à-vis other reporting dealers. Gross market values have been calculated as the sum of the total gross positive market value of contracts and the absolute value of the gross negative market value of contracts with nonreporting counterparties.

[2]Residual maturity.

[3]Counting both currency sides of each foreign exchange transaction means that the currency breakdown sums to twice the aggregate.

[4]Data before end-June 1999 refer to legacy currencies of the euro.

[5]Single-currency contracts only.

[6]Adjustments for double-counting are estimated.

[7]For end-June 1998: positions reported by institutions that only participated in the 1998 Triennial Survey of Foreign Exchange and Derivatives Market Activity; for subsequent periods: estimated positions of those institutions.

Figure 3.1 Notional Principal Amounts Outstanding for Exchange-Traded and Over-the-Counter Derivative Instruments, 1987–99

(Billions of U.S. dollars; end-year data)

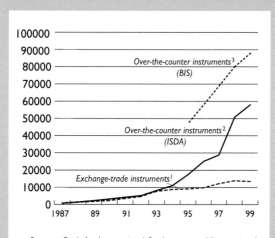

Sources: Bank for International Settlements; and International Swaps and Derivatives Association, Inc.

¹Consisting of interest-rate, currency, and stock market index futures and options.

²ISDA data, interest-rate and currency swaps (adjusted for double-counting) and interest-rate potions (consisting of caps, collars, floors, and swaptions).

³BIS data for 1995 and 1998–99.

These participants in OTC derivatives markets play one (or more) of three roles. Brokers match buyers and sellers, but avoid market and counterparty risk exposures.[14] Dealers make markets, hold inventory, and usually carry net exposure. Endusers hedge, arbitrage, or speculate. These roles have evolved over time. For example, the swap market has developed in three stages: first, a brokered market in which banks strictly intermediated trades; second, a market in which banks temporarily 'warehoused' swaps (sometimes hedging in futures markets) while they sought an offsetting exposure; and third, the current structure in which major banks and securities houses actively deal.

Derivatives Contract Structures

Both exchange-traded and OTC contracts facilitate the unbundling and transformation of financial risks such as interest rate and currency risk in broadly similar ways (see Box 3.2: Motives for OTC Derivatives Transactions). However, exchange-traded contracts have rigid structures compared with OTC derivatives contracts. For example, the Chicago Board of Trade's treasury bond futures contract dictates (1) how many treasury bonds must be delivered on each futures contract; (2) the types of treasury bonds acceptable for delivery; (3) the way prices are quoted; (4) the minimum trade-to-trade price change; (5) the months in which contracts expire; and (6) how treasury bonds are delivered from the seller of the contract to the buyer.[15] By contrast, OTC derivatives contracts can involve any underlying index, maturity, and payoff structure. OTC contracts can fill the gaps where exchange-traded contracts do not exist, including: exotic currencies and indices; customized structures (see Box 3.3: Exotic Options); and maturities that are tailored to other financial transactions. Nonetheless, some OTC derivatives instruments have become "commoditized," as market conventions and de facto standards for payments frequencies, maturities, and underlying indexes have emerged. About two-thirds of OTC derivatives' gross market value is accounted for by simple contract structures, many of which could be traded on an exchange except for minor differences in matu-

percent of the U.S. banking system's notional derivatives exposure.[12] Other kinds of financial institutions are also actively involved in some segments. In the United States, several large insurance companies have played an active role in the interest-rate segment. Some lower-rated financial institutions have used Derivatives Products Companies (DPCs) to access the market (see Box 3.1: Derivatives Products Companies). Hedge funds have been active in some segments as well, though their role may have diminished somewhat in the recent period.[13] For example, the increase in swap spreads since the 1998 mature-markets turbulence may reflect a withdrawal of liquidity by hedge funds.

---

[12]United States, Office of the Comptroller of the Currency (2000), p. 1.

[13]It recently has been noted that "hedge funds supply very necessary liquidity [in the credit derivatives market]. In many ways they are the bedrock of many modern derivative markets" (Mahtani, 1999, p. 90).

---

[14]These are distinct from the formal regulatory definitions as applied by, e.g. the U.S. Securities and Exchange Commission.

[15]Some exchange-traded contracts, such as the 'flex options' traded on the Chicago Board Options Exchange and Chicago Board of Trade, permit traders to customize aspects such as the expiration date and exercise price, but most exchange-traded contracts have a limited set of specifications.

Figure 3.2. Structure of the Over-the-Counter (OTC) Derivatives Markets, End-June 2000[1]

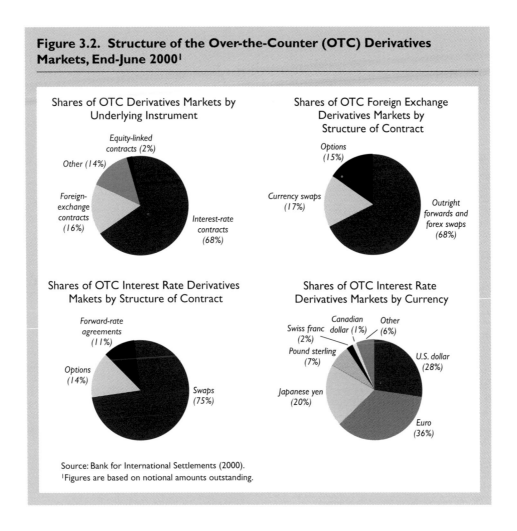

Shares of OTC Derivatives Markets by Underlying Instrument

Equity-linked contracts (2%)
Other (14%)
Foreign-exchange contracts (16%)
Interest-rate contracts (68%)

Shares of OTC Foreign Exchange Derivatives Markets by Structure of Contract

Options (15%)
Currency swaps (17%)
Outright forwards and forex swaps (68%)

Shares of OTC Interest Rate Derivatives Makets by Structure of Contract

Forward-rate agreements (11%)
Options (14%)
Swaps (75%)

Shares of OTC Interest Rate Derivatives Markets by Currency

Swiss franc (2%)
Canadian dollar (1%)
Other (6%)
Pound sterling (7%)
U.S. dollar (28%)
Japanese yen (20%)
Euro (36%)

Source: Bank for International Settlements (2000).
[1]Figures are based on notional amounts outstanding.

rity dates, notional amounts, and underlying indexes (see below).

The limited flexibility of exchange-traded contracts may partly reflect the fact that such contracts are regulated, often by both a regulatory authority and an exchange's self-regulatory organization. According to market participants, in the exchange environment, regulatory authorities evaluate proposed new contracts in a time-consuming and costly process. In the United States, the Securities and Exchange Commission (SEC) regulates exchange-traded derivatives that are legally "securities" (for example, certain options); the Commodity Futures Trading Commission (CFTC) regulates those that are legally "commodities" (for example, financial futures). Regulations promote investor protection, as exchange members act as agents for customers; market integrity, against the potential for manipulation when supplies of underlying goods, securities or commodities are limited; and efficient price discovery, an important function of

exchange-traded derivatives.[16] By contrast, OTC derivatives instruments are lightly and indirectly regulated, often because they fall between regulatory gaps. In the United States, for example, swaps contracts are classified neither as "securities" nor as "commodities," and so are regulated neither by the SEC nor the CFTC. Many justifications for regulating exchange-traded derivatives contracts are not relevant for OTC derivatives. As was recognized by U.S. courts (*Procter & Gamble v. Bankers Trust*), they are principal-to-principal agreements between sophisticated counterparties, and investor protection is not regarded as an important issue. In addition, there is minimal risk of manipulation in OTC derivatives markets, since OTC derivatives contracts do not serve a price-discovery role as do exchange-traded derivatives contracts.[17]

---

[16]See United States, President's Working Group on Financial Markets (1999b).
[17]See Greenspan (2000).

Table 3.3. Geographical Distribution of Reported Over-the-Counter (OTC) Derivatives Market Activity, April 1995 and April 1998[1]

(Average daily turnover in billions of U.S. dollars)

	Total		Foreign Exchange[2]		Interest Rate[3]	
	April 1995	April 1998	April 1995	April 1998	April 1995	April 1998
United Kingdom	351.2	591.2	292.4	468.3	58.8	122.9
United States	163.6	293.8	131.8	235.4	31.7	58.4
Japan	138.6	123.3	112.2	91.7	26.4	31.6
France	54.9	98.5	36.1	57.9	18.8	40.6
Singapore	79.2	90.7	63.0	85.4	16.3	5.3
Germany	56.0	86.7	45.1	57.6	10.9	29.1
Switzerland	46.7	63.0	44.2	57.2	2.4	5.9
Hong Kong	59.9	51.4	56.4	48.9	3.5	2.4
Canada	23.1	33.6	18.7	27.2	4.4	6.4
Australia	25.7	31.6	22.9	28.8	2.8	2.8
Other	162.6	220.6	130.2	182.3	32.6	38.2
Total "net-gross" turnover	1,161.5	1,684.4	953.0	1,340.7	208.6	343.6

Source: Bank for International Settlements, 1999, *Central Bank Survey of Foreign Exchange and Derivatives Market Activity 1998* (Basel, May).

[1]Adjusted for local double-counting ("net-gross"). It is estimated that the survey covered from 73 percent to 100 percent of derivatives markets in individual countries.

[2]Including outright forwards and foreign exchange swaps.

[3]Single-currency contracts only.

Derivatives contracts, whether exchange-traded or OTC, can be decomposed into portfolios of futures (or their OTC analog, forwards) and options. Forwards, like exchange-traded futures, convey a commitment to deliver a particular good or security at a future date at an agreed price (often settled in cash). Options (either OTC or exchange-traded) convey the right but not the obligation to buy or sell a particular good or security (often cash-settled as well). Swaps, which are an important part of the OTC derivatives markets, can be thought of as portfolios of forward contracts. Swaps exchange cashflows indexed to interest rates, foreign exchange rates, equity prices, credit instruments, or commodity prices; accordingly, swaps are often used to transform cashflows related to debt, by converting fixed-rate debt to floating-rate debt or converting yen debt to dollar debt. In addition, there are a variety of actively traded derivatives on swaps. Examples include swaptions, or options on swaps, that convey the right, but not the obligation, to enter into a swap; and forward swaps, or swaps that become activated after a certain amount of time has passed. Swaps sometimes include option-like features that allow them to be canceled or extended.

Swaps are as varied as the trading and hedging needs of market participants. Some swaps involve the exchange of payments in a single currency. In an interest rate swap, counterparties exchange interest payments on some notional amount. For example, a "vanilla" (standard) fixed-for-floating U.S. dollar interest rate swap might pay fixed interest at 6 percent and receive 6-month U.S. dollar LIBOR on a notional principal of $1 million, with the LIBOR rate reset at 6-month intervals. There are numerous variations on this basic theme.[18] Basis swaps exchange two floating-rate payments, say, LIBOR and the Federal Funds rate. Alternatively, notional principal may amortize over time, either according to a fixed schedule (an amortizing swap) or based on the evolution of an index (an index amortizing swap). In a quanto or diff swap, payments are referenced to interest rates in two currencies, but made in a single currency. For example, payments may be referenced to dollar and yen interest rates, but made only in dollars. Other swaps involve the explicit exchange of payments in

---

[18]Marshall and Kapner (1993) describe numerous varieties of swaps.

Box 3.1. Derivatives Products Companies

Concerns about counterparty risk have prompted some major financial institutions to set up special subsidiaries, known as Derivatives Products Companies (DPCs), to handle derivatives activities.[1] DPCs are structured to obtain higher ratings than the parent company, so that they can serve as the parent's vehicle for derivatives trading. A DPC is designed to insulate its counterparties from the credit risk associated with its parent: in the event of the parent's default, the parent's creditors cannot lay claim to the DPC's assets. These vehicles pass the market risk in derivatives transactions to the parent company by entering offsetting "mirror transactions" with the parent. For example, when the DPC enters a swap to pay fixed interest and receive floating interest with a counterparty, it also enters a swap to receive fixed interest and pay floating interest with its parent.

DPCs have very simple financial structures. They typically hold derivatives, cash, treasury bills, and capital. Ratings agencies require them to hold substantial resources (including initial capital, surety bonds from monoline insurers, and receivables) to earn a high rating. In addition, they operate under predefined termination procedures in the event that, for example, the DPC or its parent is downgraded or the parent defaults. There are two such procedures: contingent manager (or

continuation) structures, and early termination. Under the contingent manager or continuation structure, the DPC enters no new contracts after the termination event, but continues to service its current contracts under a prespecified contingent manager, until all its contracts mature. Under the early termination structure, the DPC accelerates its positions by unwinding them under prespecified terms. These structures—what Kroszner (1999) calls "prepackaged bankruptcy procedures"—relieve a significant degree of the uncertainty about the disposition of derivatives trades vis-à-vis such a counterparty in the event of default.

DPCs came into existence in the early 1990s, amid increasing concerns about counterparty credit risk stemming from the recession and the bankruptcy of Drexel Burnham Lambert. Since then, they have garnered only a relatively small share of the business. According to recent estimates, the major DPCs account for about $1.7 trillion in notional principal, only about 2 percent of global outstandings. Moreover, the popularity of DPCs has waned in more recent years (in fact, two institutions have recently closed their DPCs), as the credit ratings of many major banks and securities firms have improved and as more multiproduct collateral and netting agreements have been put in place. The vehicle remains attractive for lower-rated institutions; a major Japanese securities house recently considered establishing a DPC in order to make inroads into the global derivatives market.

---

[1]See Remolona, Bassett, and In Sun (1996) and Kroszner (1999).

---

two different currencies. Currency swaps provide for the periodic exchange of interest payments in two currencies as well as initial and final exchange of principal. In foreign exchange swaps, principal amounts are exchanged at initiation and maturity, while in cross-currency interest rate swaps, only interest-rate payments in the two reference currencies are exchanged.

Other OTC derivatives include structured notes, which link interest and principal to an index, and credit derivatives. Structured notes have interest and principal payments that are linked to an underlying index. The index and its relationship to cashflows are as varied as the hedging needs or risk appetites of the counterparties. For example, consider a structured note involving the Mexican peso (with all cashflows in dollars).[19] The note might pay an 85 percent coupon and principal that decreases by 5 percent for every 1 percent depreciation in the peso between inception and maturity. Such a note is equivalent to a dollar loan that is leveraged

fourfold into a peso deposit. Although the note is effectively a highly-leveraged foreign-currency investment, under 1994 Mexican prudential regulations the transaction would have appeared for regulatory purposes as a peso investment. Such structures have been particularly popular for circumventing regulations, for example, on foreign-currency investment.

Credit derivatives are indexed to the total return of an underlying security, to a credit event, or to credit spreads.[20] A total return swap exchanges fixed or floating interest (say, LIBOR plus a spread) for the total return on a reference security (interest or dividend payments plus price appreciation or depreciation). A credit default swap exchanges a fee for an agreement to cover the loss on a reference security if a predefined credit event occurs. A credit linked note pays interest and principal until a credit event occurs; its payment is then linked to the recovery value of a reference asset. The market for

---

[19]Steinherr (1998, p. 117).

[20]See Smithson and Hayt (1999), pp. 54–55. Credit events include default or a downgrade to sub-investment grade.

Box 3.2. Motives for OTC Derivatives Transactions

While OTC derivatives in the form of forward sales of agricultural goods date back to the 15th century, and perhaps earlier (the first options trade is attributed to the Greek philosopher Thales circa 600 B.C.), the modern forms of OTC derivatives originated in incentives from three sources: economic incentives, including the need to share and hedge risk; restrictions on financial activity, including regulation, investment restrictions, and taxation of financial transactions; and the internationalization of finance and the associated technological and methodological advances. Three historical examples illustrating the use of OTC derivatives show how these incentives shaped OTC derivatives markets.

First, the market for interest rate swaps grew out of a desire to exploit differential interest rate advantages for borrowing at fixed versus floating rates. For example, suppose a low-rated bank has to pay 100 basis points more than a high-rated bank when borrowing at fixed rates, while it has to pay only 10 basis points more than the high-rated bank when borrowing at floating rates. In this case, the two banks could profit from each bank's comparative advantage: the low-rated bank would borrow at floating rates, the top-rated bank would borrow at fixed rates, and both banks would exchange the cash flows.[1] These types of transactions gave rise to the interest rate swap market. Initially, banks and other financial institutions served as brokers by matching buyers and sellers for a fee. But this activity ultimately evolved into the current OTC derivatives markets in which the internationally active commercial and investment banks actively trade and manage very large portfolios of swaps, including for their own proprietary accounts. Interest rate swaps presently account for about two-thirds of OTC derivatives markets activity in interest rate contracts.

Second, consider the market for currency swaps. These derivatives instruments arose from a need by multinationals to make foreign currency investments in the presence of policy measures designed to discourage capital outflows and thus limit pressures on exchange rates. For example, in the 1970s, the U.K. government imposed taxes on sterling foreign exchange transactions. As a result, it was more costly to borrow dollars in London than in New York. Multinational corporations set up parallel and back-to-back loans to circumvent the tax and lower the cost to U.K. companies of borrowing dollars.[2] These arrangements avoided the tax on foreign exchange transactions, because each leg involved the U.S. and U.K. companies borrowing and lending dollars in the United States and sterling in the United Kingdom. The modern currency-swap markets developed as companies seeking to engage in these transactions turned to the major financial institutions to find overseas counterparts with matching interests. Now these markets are used for a variety of commercial purposes, including arbitraging differences in national interest rates.

Third, take, for example, the market for credit derivatives (which are indexed to credit risk). For many financial institutions, the bulk of financial risk is credit risk. Credit derivatives permit these institutions to adjust their credit risk profiles and increase the efficiency of their economic and regulatory capital.[3] By using a credit derivative, for example, the holder of a sovereign bond can mitigate the risk of sovereign default and retain the currency and interest rate risk. Credit derivatives are presently a small share of the overall market, but promise strong growth in the future and may come to play a key role in pricing, trading, and managing credit risk.

---

[1]See Lau (1997), p. 26. An alternative interpretation of this "pure" comparative advantage swap is that it transfers the credit risk to the high-rated borrower.

[2]The eurodollar market emerged in the 1960s partly in response to the U.S. Interest Equalization Tax and the Foreign Credit Restraint Program; see Grabbe (1991), p. 14.

[3]One major institution reportedly has used credit derivatives to halve the economic capital absorbed by its credit portfolio. See Smith (2000), p. v.

---

credit derivatives is currently small—notional value was recently estimated at around $650 billion, compared with about $80 trillion for all OTC derivatives—but promises strong future growth. Credit derivatives are still in the early stages of the derivatives 'product cycle,' which is driven by client needs, technology, regulatory and tax considerations, and market conditions. As many of these factors become more favorable to the development of the market, and as banks seek to liquify credit exposures on their balance sheets (blurring the distinction between securitization and the use of credit derivatives) and develop and make markets in credit

risk, credit derivatives may come to play a central role in the management of credit risk. In the near term, challenges in documenting credit-derivatives trades, the inability to offset some kinds of risks for regulatory capital requirements, and concerns that banks may use their superior information about credit risk to the disadvantage of clients may work to limit growth in this nascent market segment of global derivative markets. There are also important legal uncertainties about the performance of credit derivatives in the event of counterparty bankruptcy, in part because credit derivatives are, under current law, junior to other claims. Meanwhile, the market

Box 3.3. Exotic Options

The flexibility of OTC derivatives contracts allows unusual contract structures to be traded, including in options.[1] In a standard option, the buyer pays a fee (premium) up front, and receives an option to either buy (call option) or sell (put option) the underlying security at a specified price (strike price). This right may be exercisable only at maturity (European option) or at any time up until maturity (American option). At exercise, the payoff to the option is the difference between the strike price and the price of the underlying security (its intrinsic value). Options with simple structures such as these are known as "vanilla" options.

Exotic options can change any or all of these features:

- The option may be exercisable at several fixed points in time (Bermuda option).
- The premium can be paid at maturity, rather than at initiation (break forward, Boston option).
- The option can start with a delay (forward start option), as with some employee incentive stock options.
- The underlying can be another option, rather than an underlying security (compound options); for example, an option on an interest-rate cap (caption) or floor (floortion).
- The underlying may be another derivative, for example, a swap (swaption).
- The holder may pick at some point whether the option is a call or put option (chooser option).
- Barrier options are canceled (knockout) or activated (knock-in) when a price threshold is crossed.
- Binary options pay a fixed amount (cash or nothing option) or full asset value (asset or nothing option).
- The payoff may depend on the maximum or minimum price attained by the underlying (look back option) or on the average price of the underlying during the life of the option (Asian option).

- During the contract's life, the holder may be able to pick a day, and at expiration receive the maximum of the intrinsic value on that day and the intrinsic value at maturity (shout option).
- The payoff may depend on the prices of several underlying securities (rainbow, basket, exchange options).
- The option may have a payoff that is nonlinear in the underlying price (power caps).
- The option's payoff may be denominated in a different currency than the underlying (quanto).
- Many variations either combine one or more of these features, or amount to portfolios of options.

Exotic options raise a number of challenges for the financial institutions that trade them. They can be exceedingly challenging to price; options for which the payoff depends on the price history may not have a closed form solution for the price. In addition, they can be very challenging to hedge. Options are traditionally dynamically hedged by holding a quantity of the underlying security, which is periodically adjusted for changes in the price of the underlying security.[2] How much of the underlying security is held depends upon how the option's price responds to changes in the underlying; this response can change dramatically for exotic options. Suppose, for example, that when the price of the underlying security rises by one dollar, the price of an option on one unit of the underlying rises by 50 cents; in market parlance, the option's delta (change with respect to the underlying) is 0.5. A portfolio of two options, and one unit of the underlying, is then perfectly hedged. However, the value of delta changes with the price of the underlying security. For knockout options, the value of delta declines sharply to zero as the barrier is approached. This has the potential to suddenly unbalance the hedged position and cause a sudden rush of sales or purchases of the underlying security to rebalance the portfolio.

---

[1]See, for example, Hull (2000), Chapter 18. These "exotic" structures may be nonstandard and complex, but they are not necessarily rare, thinly traded, or especially risky.

[2]Another approach is to hedge using a portfolio of other options constructed to automatically adjust for changes in the price of the underlying security (static hedging).

---

may be driven by trading activity rather than hedging; in fact, it may be easier to trade a credit derivative on a bond than the bond itself.

OTC and exchange markets are viewed by market participants as existing in parallel, and OTC contracts are hedged by using standard, exchange-traded derivatives. Moreover, derivatives on the same underlying risk are sometimes traded both over the counter and on exchanges: for example,

options on major currencies are traded over the counter and on the Philadelphia Exchange, and a variety of interest-rate contracts are traded both on exchanges and OTC. The major participants who benefit most from OTC derivatives markets envision that exchange-traded derivatives will remain an important part of their risk management toolbox, and that organized exchange markets will continue to exist alongside OTC markets.

Exchange Versus Over-the-Counter Market Structures

A comparison of the market structures for OTC and exchange-traded derivatives can provide a useful perspective on important features of OTC derivatives markets. Compared with exchange-traded derivatives markets, OTC derivatives markets have the following features: management of counterparty (credit) risk is decentralized and located within individual institutions; there are no formal centralized limits on individual positions, leverage, or margining; there are no formal rules for risk and burden-sharing; and there are no formal rules or mechanisms for ensuring market stability and integrity, or for safeguarding the collective interests of market participants.

Organization of Derivatives Trading and Corresponding Frameworks for Promoting Market Stability

Apart from contract flexibility, the most salient differences between OTC and exchange-traded derivatives lie in the organization of trading and the corresponding frameworks for promoting market stability. Trading, clearing and settlement, risk management, and contingency management (handling a clearing-member default, for example) are highly formalized and centralized in exchange markets, but are informal, bilateral, and comparatively decentralized in OTC markets.

Organized Exchange Markets: Centralized, Formal, Regulated, Rule-Driven

Organized exchange trading has four main components: membership requirements; rules governing conduct (including risk management); centralized trading, clearing, and settlement; and rules that mutualize risk, including loss-sharing in case of defaults. These rules are designed to ensure market integrity, promote efficient price discovery, and safeguard the resources of the clearinghouse. A clearinghouse may be part of the exchange, or a separate legal entity. Exchange members normally commit capital or have an ownership interest in the clearinghouse.

In order to maintain market stability and financial integrity, exchanges impose soundness, disclosure, transparency, and prudential requirements on members. Typically, there are minimum capital requirements, protection of customer funds, reporting, and compliance with other rules and regulations. Exchanges closely monitor trading activity with a view to identifying large customer positions or concentrations of positions. They also promote transparency by reporting positions, turnover, and price data, and determining settlement prices, usually on a daily basis. Following the collapse of Barings, some clearinghouses share information and assess members' net exposures across markets.[21]

The clearinghouse manages credit risk and is the central legal counterparty to every transaction; it has a matched market-risk position, but has current credit exposures. Credit risk arises because a change in the price of the underlying asset could cause one counterparty to owe a considerable amount on its position, particularly if the contract is highly leveraged. If an exchange member defaults, the clearinghouse normally has the right to liquidate the member's positions, take the member's security deposit, margin, and performance bonds, attach certain other member assets, and invoke any guarantee from the member's parent company. If the defaulting member's resources cannot cover the obligation, the exchange can normally turn to the resources of other clearing members by invoking loss-sharing rules. In the event of member default, most clearinghouses transfer the member's client positions to another member; a few close out the client positions and liquidate the margin. Exchanges also have backup credit lines.[22] Clearinghouse defaults have been exceedingly rare.

Most importantly, exchanges formalize risk-management and loss-sharing rules designed to protect the exchange's capital and the capital of its members. Members are usually, but not always, required to keep speculative positions within strictly defined limits, mark to market at least daily, and post initial and variation margin to limit the exchange's net credit exposure to the member. Members are subject to surprise inspections and surveys of their financial condition, compliance with exchange rules, and risk-management abilities. Likewise, there are rules that protect the exchange and its members from trading activities of nonmembers, which must trade through members. For example, on some exchanges, members of the exchange need not be members of the clearinghouse, but trades must be cleared through clearinghouse members. Exchanges also dictate minimum margin requirements for member exposures to clients (often higher than the requirements for members), as well as client position limits. In addition, clearing members handling clients' accounts may face more stringent capital requirements compared with those only trading on their own account.

---

[21]See Steinherr (1998), p. 180.
[22]See Kroszner (1999).

OTC Markets: Decentralized, Informal, Lightly Supervised and Regulated, Market-Discipline-Driven

By contrast, OTC derivatives markets lack a formal structure. There are no membership criteria, but counterparties prefer to deal only with highly rated and well-capitalized intermediaries to minimize counterparty risk. OTC derivatives markets are similar to interbank and interdealer markets. They comprise an informal network of bilateral relationships and there is no physical central trading place. Instead, the OTC derivatives markets exist on the collective trading floors of the major financial institutions. There is no central mechanism to limit individual or aggregate risk taking, leverage, and credit extension, and risk management is completely decentralized. Market participants individually perform risk management, in particular the management of the credit risk in the bilateral, principal-to-principal agreements, which is particularly challenging because exposures vary with the price of the underlying security and can rise very sharply.

The operational aspects of OTC derivatives markets are also decentralized. There is no centralized trading, clearing, or settlement mechanism in OTC markets. Transparency is generally limited as well. Except for semiannual central-bank surveys, market participants do not report outstanding positions or prices for aggregation or dissemination. Information about market concentration and who owns which risks is generally unavailable; at best, a trading desk might know that some institutions are building up positions. This lack of transparency enabled LTCM to build up outsized positions during 1997 and 1998.[23]

As discussed in more detail in Section IV, OTC instruments and trading are essentially unregulated, although they are affected indirectly by national legal systems, regulations, banking supervision, and market surveillance. None of the major financial centers has an "OTC derivatives regulator" similar to a banking or a securities regulator.[24] Nor is the institutional coverage comprehensive, as hedge funds and unregulated securities affiliates are not regulated. Regulations are also highly fragmented, both nationally and internationally. In the United States, for example, there are at least three groups of regulators—securities, commodity futures, and banking—impinging on OTC derivatives activities. In addition, while the major market-making institutions flexibly book

trades around the globe, supervision and regulation are nationally oriented. Nevertheless, despite its limited role, the current regulatory framework has had a visible impact on the market.

This light regulation and supervision exists alongside a set of private mechanisms that facilitate smoothly functioning OTC derivatives markets. Market discipline, provided by shareholders and creditors, promotes market stability by rewarding financial institutions based on their performance and creditworthiness. Recent research finds market discipline to be strong only during periods of banking sector stress and volatile financial markets.[25]

Market discipline is present when a firm's private sector financial stakeholders (shareholders, creditors, and counterparties) are at risk of financial loss from the firm's decisions and can take actions to "discipline" the firm and to influence its behavior. Market discipline may operate through share price movements, by constraining the supply of credit, or through the willingness to do business through counterparty relationships. Market discipline in financial markets therefore rests on two key elements: investors' ability to accurately assess a firm's financial condition ("monitoring") and the responsiveness of the firm's management to investor feedback ("influence").[26] Institutions mark their trading books to market daily so that unprofitable decisions and poor risk management can be reflected immediately in measured performance (profits and losses). This informs senior management and, through disclosure, financial stakeholders. These mechanisms have some influence, as demonstrated during the turbulence in 1998 when those institutions that appeared to manage well enjoyed the most buoyant stock prices, and creditors of institutions perceived to be less creditworthy refused to roll over credit lines or bond issues, and sold their credit instruments in the secondary market. The subsequent reductions in proprietary trading activity seem to have been largely motivated by financial stakeholders' desire for less risky earnings.

In OTC derivatives markets, special obstacles for effective market discipline (both "monitoring" and "influence") tend to be related to information disclosure—one of the fundamental preconditions for effective market discipline. For example, the off-balance-sheet character of derivatives makes it difficult for outside financial stakeholders to evaluate the financial health of an institution and its contingent liabilities. Data on individual exposures is proprietary, and disclosure could diminish potential

---

[23]See International Monetary Fund (1999), Chapter IV.

[24]Among the exceptions, in Brazil all OTC derivatives transactions must be centrally registered. See United States, Commodity Futures Trading Commission (1999), pp. 64–65.

[25]See Covitz, Hancock, and Kwast (2000).

[26]See United States, Board of Governors of the Federal Reserve Board (1999).

profits. In addition, competitive pressures and the desire to see order flows can lead creditors to extend credit without insisting on adequate counterparty disclosure, as occurred, for example, with LTCM. Therefore, more emphasis may have to be placed on counterparty monitoring, as there may be significant limits to broader market discipline for complex institutions that are active in the OTC derivatives markets.

Supplementing these mechanisms, a number of industry groups are involved in initiatives designed to support well-functioning OTC derivatives markets, notably the International Swaps and Derivatives Association (ISDA), the Counterparty Risk Management Policy Group, the Group of 30, and the Derivatives Policy Group. Efforts include dissemination of best practices in risk management; standardization of documentation; identification of gaps in risk-management practices, and flaws in the operational infrastructure; assessments of legal and other operational risks; efforts to foster interindustry and public/private dialogues on key issues; and initiatives to voluntarily disclose information to regulatory authorities. The activities of these groups reflect the fact that market participants see it as in their best interest to encourage an orderly, effective, and efficient market, and also to discourage regulation.

Corporate governance monitoring by financial stakeholders and private initiatives imposes discipline on OTC derivatives activities and increases incentives to reflect the degree of counterparty risk in pricing, margins, or collateral. They also create benchmarks against which participants, end-users, and regulators can measure progress in dealing with the issues raised in public and private forums. Some of the same factors that complicate market discipline (such as the opacity of OTC derivatives) are also the very factors that make market discipline desirable from the standpoint of financial regulators.

To summarize, OTC derivatives markets and activities are highly decentralized and lightly regulated compared with exchange markets and activities. The decentralized and informal structure of OTC derivatives activities and the indirect impact of the regulatory environment are reflected in the day-to-day operational and risk management practices of its major participants. These practices are described next.

Trading and Back-Office Infrastructure for OTC Derivatives Dealing

Like other trades, OTC derivatives trades are initiated in the front-office trading function, then cleared, managed, and settled in the middle- and back-office functions (Figure 3.3 and Box 3.4: The Life of a Two-Year Interest-Rate Swap).[27] Although market terminology does not always precisely distinguish back-office from middle-office functions, firms increasingly describe risk management as a "middle-office" function, distinct from "back-office" activities such as clearing and settlement (though back-office functions can have risk-management aspects as well, for example, by mitigating operational risk). That distinction is followed here.

The Trading Function

The first step of an OTC derivatives trade is soliciting a price. Prices are normally quoted bilaterally within an informal network of familiar counterparties, usually over the telephone or over electronic quoting or broking systems. Screen-based prices are prevalent in "vanilla" segments such as interest-rate swaps and options and foreign-exchange forwards, though market participants may not be able to readily transact at these prices (owing in part to CFTC restrictions described in Section IV).[28] Even when bid and offer prices are posted—as in the swaps market—these are generally indications for "vanilla" deals with the highest-rated counterparties. "Non-vanilla" or off-market swaps that involve amortizing or accreting principal, a nonstandard fixed-rate coupon or floating rate index, or other adjustments often require a customized quote. Nonetheless, trading arrangements are becoming more formalized in a few segments of the OTC derivatives market. In 1999, Derivatives Net Inc. announced a new system for swaps trading ("Blackbird"); three brokers began to set up an electronic broking systems for swaps and other fixed-income derivatives; and the CreditTrade system for credit derivatives began operation (Creditex, another electronic trading system for credit derivatives, began operation in March 2000).

Since a trade implies a current or potential increase in counterparty risk exposure, most firms check credit limits and other risk controls before finalizing the trade. The trader may check an internal reporting system or consult a risk or relationship manager. Once the trade has been checked for consistency with risk limits and confirmed informally,

---

[27]Market terminology in this area is imprecise; some refer to clearing and settlement as "clearing," particularly when one institution (a clearing corporation) performs both functions.

[28]Foreign-exchange derivatives are an exception as they have been traded on electronic systems for some time. In 1999, only two of 16 jurisdictions surveyed indicated that multilateral electronic execution facilities are available for OTC transactions (see United States, Commodity Futures Trading Commission (1999)).

Figure 3.3 The Life of an OTC Derivatives Trade

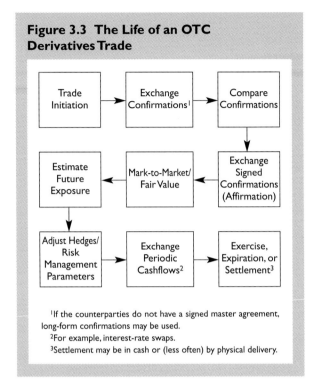

[1] If the counterparties do not have a signed master agreement, long-form confirmations may be used.

[2] For example, interest-rate swaps.

[3] Settlement may be in cash or (less often) by physical delivery.

more formal confirmation and clearing usually takes place in the back office.[29]

Back-Office Infrastructure

The back office provides five critical functions: issuing and monitoring confirmations; recording transactions; settling transactions; ensuring that legal documentation is completed; and producing information for management and control purposes, including reports on positions that are subject to trading and counterparty limits, reports on profitability, and reports on exceptions that require action (unsigned confirmations and breaches of limits, for example).[30]

Clearing is a particularly important back-office function. Trade confirmations form a critical part of this process. Interbank counterparties normally exchange, by fax or telex, confirmation letters detailing the economic terms of the trade and other particulars within one to five days of the trade. When counterparties have not yet signed a master agree-

ment (described below), the confirmation letter often describes closeout netting arrangements; these are called long-form confirmations. In brokered trades, the broker may issue confirmations to both parties. In transactions with nonbank end-users, it is common that only the bank counterparty sends a confirmation. The back office checks the terms of the confirmation to ensure that both parties agree to the same terms; discrepancies crop up in 5 to 10 percent of trades.

Trade capture, in which the details of the trade are entered in management information systems, can be cumbersome for OTC derivatives dealers. First, large dealers—and even active end-users—have many counterparties and positions: for example, LTCM had some 50 counterparties in the OTC derivatives markets, and was counterparty to tens of thousands of transactions in all markets. Second, some OTC derivatives products have complex terms. While a cash instrument may be described by two or three parameters or a simple security identifier, a complex derivative instrument requires pages of documentation. Trade capture takes seconds for foreign exchange and cash trades, compared with up to two hours for complex trades. As a result of these complexities, traders frequently record the wrong interest rate, term, or counterparty in trade information systems. Errors early in the process can compound later; the trade information system may fail to inform the trader that an in-the-money option is expiring, or that a counterparty has missed several payments.[31] For this reason, risk managers see it as critical to detect and fix errors early in the process, and see managing the first day of the trade as key. Errors are usually caught and corrected early in the trade capture cycle and they are therefore not generally viewed as 'life-threatening.'

The back office also tracks and records the value of OTC derivatives transactions and positions. First, it checks and corrects the price data submitted by the trading desk. Once the data have been "scrubbed," they are used to value the firm's positions, and to calculate profit, loss, and exposures. The precise way that OTC derivatives transactions and exposures translate into gains, losses, and exposures on the income statement and balance sheet depends on a number of factors, including the jurisdiction and whether the derivatives are used for hedging or trading.

Valuation of OTC derivatives raises special challenges for the back office. Following Statement 133 by the Financial Accounting Standards Board (FASB) and IASC International Accounting Standard 39, OTC derivatives are often recorded at fair value, which the FASB has defined as "the amount at which

---

[29] Informal confirmation often takes place over the telephone. Whether a verbal agreement creates a binding contract or not (in the United Kingdom, it does; elsewhere, it is less clear), firms typically tape phone conversations and store the tapes for six months to one year after the conversation takes place.

[30] See Global Derivatives Study Group (1993), p. 69.

[31] An option is "in the money" when it is profitable to exercise.

Box 3.4. The Life of a Two-Year Interest-Rate Swap

Suppose that a company owns a $100 million, two-year bond that pays semiannual fixed interest at 10 percent, but would prefer a floating-rate bond. Instead of selling the fixed-rate bond and buying a floating-rate bond, it can convert the fixed-rate bond's cashflows from fixed to floating by entering with an intermediary into a two-year interest-rate swap in which it pays a fixed rate of interest and receives a floating rate (for dollar-denominated interest-rate swaps, the floating-rate index is often LIBOR, or the rate on Treasury bills, commercial paper, or federal funds). In this case, the company will be the "fixed-rate payer" and the intermediary will be the "fixed-rate receiver."

The company phones an intermediary to obtain a quote on such a swap. Swap rates are normally quoted by reference to the interest rate on the fixed leg of the transaction and expressed as a spread over Treasury rates. The intermediary offers to pay LIBOR flat in return for 8 percent fixed interest. The rate of 8 percent is then the swap rate or swap coupon on this two-year swap. The swap rate is normally expressed as the semiannual yield to maturity on the fixed rate leg against a flat floating rate. It is typically quoted in terms of a spread to Treasury rates of the same maturity. Suppose that the two-year Treasury note yields 7.75 percent. The swap spread quoted to the company is then 25 basis points.

Swap rates may be either on market—that is, calculated using prevailing interest rates and with a standard payment frequency, notional amount, and floating-rate index—or off market, with one or more of these aspects customized (standardized swaps are also known as "plain vanilla" swaps). For short-dated, U.S. dollar interest rate swaps, on-market swap rates are calculated from eurodollar futures rates. For this two-year swap, the intermediary would first compound the yields on eight successive three-month eurodollar contracts to arrive at the swap rate.[1] The intermediary would then add and subtract small amounts (perhaps a few basis points) to reflect credit risk and the cost of doing business to arrive at the fixed rates that it would be willing to receive and pay on swaps; the difference between the intermediary's "receive" and "pay" rates is the bid-ask spread.

If the company accepts the swap arrangement, the intermediary fills out and sends a confirmation form that spells out the details of the swap, including the floating-rate index, the frequency of payment, and any arrangement for collateral. The company checks, signs, and returns the confirmation. If the intermediary and company have a master agreement between them, the swap may be encompassed by that agreement; if not, the intermediary may use a more detailed confirmation (a long-form confirmation) that sets out many of the considerations that are normally covered in the master agreement. The date that the deal is agreed is known as the trade date; interest begins to accrue on the effective date (perhaps 5 business days later), and any initial cashflows are exchanged on the settlement date (often the same as the effective date).

The company has now in effect converted the fixed-rate bond that pays 10 percent to a floating-rate bond that pays LIBOR plus 2 percent: the company receives 10 percent from the bond, pays 8 percent on the swap, and receives LIBOR (see figure). The intermediary now may have an open exposure to interest rates, depending on the configuration of swaps and other instruments on its books. The intermediary may choose to hold the position, enter an offsetting swap (paying fixed rates and receiving floating), or hedge the position using U.S. Treasury securities or eurodollar futures.

The intermediary also enters the details of the swap into the data management system, capturing the important details in the firm's risk-management system, which would calculate the exposure to the company net of any other positions. In a standard, on-market swap, the expected present value of the swap is zero, so no cash changes hands up front. However, both the intermediary and the company have potential future exposure (PFE)

---

[1]See Marshall and Kapner (1993), Chapter 7. The two-year swap would be viewed as "short-dated" since liquid Eurodollar futures are available out to two years. Pricing long-dated swaps is more complicated; see Marshall and Kapner (1993), pp. 154–63.

---

the instrument could be exchanged in a current transaction between willing participants, other than in a forced or liquidation sale."[32] In practice, fair value may be estimated using a model of the present value of future cashflows, sometimes with adjustments for credit risk, market risk, concentration, liquidity, closeout and administration costs, or complexity. For illiquid OTC derivatives positions, valuations may also be imputed from a replicating portfolio of more liquid derivatives (for example, the value of a foreign exchange barrier option may be estimated from the value of a replicating portfolio of vanilla foreign exchange options). When models are used to mark positions, model valuations are sometimes periodically checked against market quotations.

The back-office function is also responsible for settling OTC derivatives transactions. Most OTC derivatives are cash settled or allow for it. Payments change hands during the contract's life (for interest-rate and cross-currency interest rate swaps, periodic exchange of interest, and for foreign ex-

---

[32]See Kawaller (1999).

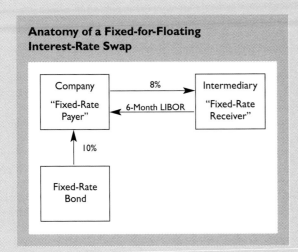

Anatomy of a Fixed-for-Floating Interest-Rate Swap

(see Box 3.5). Accordingly, one or both may have the right to take collateral up front (in arrangements like the one described, normally only the intermediary has the right to take collateral). Moreover, as market rates

change, and PFE fluctuates, both current exposure and PFE may rise, and the intermediary may make collateral calls (as well as rehedging market risk exposure).

After 6 months, the first "reset" period is reached, and the first payment is due. The size of the gross and net payments depends upon the 6-month LIBOR at the beginning of the period when the deal was struck (say, December 2000). Suppose that the 6-month LIBOR was 6 percent. The company is obligated to pay 8 percent of $100 million; the intermediary is obligated to pay 6 percent of $100 million; net, then, the company is obligated to pay the intermediary 2 percent of $100 million, or $2 million (see table). Note that the gross and net flows are considerably smaller than the notional value of $100 million. The market value of the swap would likewise be small compared with the notional value (perhaps 5 percent of the notional).

This process continues through the end of the life of the swap, at the end of the second year. At that point, the swap agreement expires, and any excess collateral is returned (in a "plain vanilla" interest rate swap, the two counterparties do not exchange principal).

Period Ending	6-month LIBOR	Fixed interest payment (from company)	Floating-rate payment (from intermediary)	Net payment (from intermediary to company)
December 2000	6 percent			
June 2001	7 percent	$8 million	$6 million	-$2 million
December 2001	8 percent	$8 million	$7 million	-$1 million
June 2002	9 percent	$8 million	$8 million	None
December 2002	...	$8 million	$9 million	$1 million

change swaps, exchange of principal at initiation and maturity). Such payments may be reduced by bilateral netting.[33] Payment risks in currency swaps are sometimes mitigated by a third-party escrow arrangement that transfers final payments to counterparties only after it has been paid by both.

Some dealers also manage settlement risks in two-way payments by specifying that counterparties pay first, before the dealer pays. Overall, except when principal is at risk (as in foreign exchange transactions), most market participants see settlement risk in OTC derivatives transactions as no greater than in cash transactions, where management of settlement risk is well developed and understood. In addition, because netting practices are widely accepted, payments associated with OTC derivatives transactions are a relatively small fraction of total gross obligations for most institutions,

---

[33]Data from the U.S. Office of the Comptroller of the Currency show that bilateral netting reduces credit exposure on derivatives among all U.S. banks by about 60 percent, and that this percentage has increased over time.

usually around five percent and no more than 15 percent of total payments.

Increasing competition and declining spreads create pressure to rationalize middle- and back-office costs. Some small to medium-sized market participants find it more economical to subcontract middle- and back-office functions to another firm, rather than perform them in-house. For example, hedge funds often employ a prime broker that handles financing, custody, recordkeeping, and clearing.[34] For larger institutions, pressures to lower costs will likely mean increased automation of back-office functions, which is limited outside the more commoditized segments.[35] In 1999, a new electronic system for checking and matching OTC derivatives confirmations (Londex) was introduced, and major market participants have signed up. There are also suggestions that SWIFT[36] may be used more extensively for electronic exchange of OTC derivatives confirmations, although SWIFT membership is limited and the SWIFT system apparently cannot handle some structured transactions.

Once the trade is confirmed, initially settled, checked, and recorded, the first part of its "life cycle" is ended. At that point, middle-office risk managers take responsibility for managing its market, credit, and operational risks.

Middle Office: Managing the Risks Associated with OTC Derivatives Positions

The principles of prudent risk management are the same in OTC derivatives as in other areas: avoid concentration, know your counterparty, manage maturity, and mark-to-market. Similarly, some of the same risk-management tools used for other types of exposures can be used for OTC derivatives as well. This section provides a general overview of the risk management considerations surrounding OTC derivatives, including those that are particular to OTC derivatives positions.

Market Risks

Market risks in OTC derivatives are managed using familiar tools such as the value-at-risk (VaR) model, which measures how much of the firm's capital could be lost owing to swings in the value of its portfolio, given a host of simplifying assumptions.[37] Recent bouts of turbulence have revealed the limitations of these simplifying assumptions. For example, standard VaR models ignore the confluence of credit and market risk, which is a key consideration for OTC derivatives exposures. Counterparty credit exposure rises when market moves put a derivatives exposure into the money (so-called "wrong-way risk"—see below). When the exposure is highly leveraged, even small market moves can give rise to large changes in credit exposure. In a five-year interest-rate swap, a 100 basis point change in rates can increase credit exposure by 400 basis points of notional principal.[38] The confluence of credit and market risk can be particularly complicated for options, as option credit exposure varies nonlinearly with the price of the underlying security.[39]

Credit Risk

Modeling of market risks is more advanced than modeling of credit exposures (including counterparty exposures) in OTC derivatives. Market risk is reasonably well approximated by means, standard deviations, and correlations, but credit risk—particularly the risk of "tail events"—requires a more refined approach, and a portfolio approach to counterparty credit risk remains elusive. Instead, counterparty credit risk is more often managed like other types of credit risk—that is, "one name at a time," using internal ratings, models of rating migration, estimates of default probabilities and expected loss from spreads on other senior unsecured claims (such as corporate bonds), and scenario analyses. A few dealers also explicitly mark to market the credit risk in their swap books, and some use instruments such as corporate bonds or credit derivatives to hedge counterparty risk in OTC derivatives exposures. As the market for credit derivatives develops further, it may provide timely market estimates of credit risk for these purposes.

One of the key concepts of counterparty credit risk in a derivatives contract is potential future exposure (PFE), or the amount potentially at risk if a counterparty defaults (see Box 3.5: Measuring Potential Future Exposure in a Swap Contract). Consider a German securities firm that buys a put option on a U.S. stock (currently trading at $300) from a U.S. bank, giving the German securities firm the right to sell the equity at $300 (the strike price). If the U.S. stock falls

---

[34]Major banks are among the providers of prime brokerage services. In March 2000, J.P. Morgan announced plans to set up a separate company (Arcordia) to offer post-trade operations associated with derivatives.

[35]See Trant (1999).

[36]SWIFT is a banking industry-owned payment and settlement messaging network that is operated by the Society for Worldwide Interbank Financial Telecommunications.

[37]See International Monetary Fund (1999), pp. 69–70.

[38]White (1997).

[39]Hull (2000), Chapter 13.

to $100, the option will be worth about $200 to the German securities firm, since it could buy the stock for $100 in the spot market, then exercise the option and sell it to the U.S. bank for $300.[40] From a market-risk perspective, the trade has worked out well so far for the German securities firm, but from a credit-risk perspective, it has become riskier. If the U.S. bank defaults on its obligation, the German securities firm stands to lose a lot more than it did at the inception of the trade. Moreover, if the drop in the price of the U.S. stock coincides with a deterioration in the U.S. bank's ability to pay—as it well might—the chance of default and the loss given default both rise sharply. This adverse confluence between market and credit risk is known as "wrong-way" risk, and caused sharp losses during recent crises.

Risk managers mitigate counterparty credit risk exposure using a variety of techniques, including: collateral; netting; concentration limits by industry and counterparty (sometimes with additional limits by maturity); periodic recouponing (resetting swap terms to return its mark-to-market value to zero); and credit triggers that give the option to force cash settlement if the counterparty's credit rating deteriorates. Payments may be made more frequently on riskier exposures (for example, monthly or quarterly rather than semi-annually). Market participants pay close attention to the maturity of their exposures, in part because exchange-traded hedging instruments generally have short maturities. Exposures tend to be concentrated at short maturities (see Table 3.2), and long-dated (for example, 20-year) swaps sometimes have an optional or mandatory unwind after 5 or 10 years.[41]

Collateral is a particularly important tool for managing counterparty risks in OTC derivatives markets. In 1999, some $175 billion to $200 billion in collateral covered credit exposures in derivatives and foreign exchange positions.[42] Large institutions averaged over 1,000 collateral arrangements and collateralized just over half of OTC derivatives trades, while midsized institutions averaged about 140 agreements and collateralized about one-third of their OTC derivatives trades. Dealers indicated that 45 percent of collateral arrangements involved other banks and broker dealers; 20 percent involved hedge funds; another 20 percent involved corporations (usually end users); 8 percent involved central banks and supranational agencies; and the remaining 7 per-

cent involved counterparties such as private individuals. In general, collateral is used much more intensively in some countries (particularly the United States) than others.[43] Dealers' willingness to take collateral depends in part on whether they can reuse it (for example, through repo) and in part on their operational capabilities to track collateral. Collateral is operationally demanding; an active dealer might mark-to-market 100,000 transactions every day.

Collateral positions are usually marked-to-market daily, though dealers do not always make daily collateral calls. Other terms that vary are the use of one-way versus two-way collateral (whether only one party, or both, potentially posts collateral) and rehypothecation (the reuse of collateral).[44] ISDA credit support annexes (CSAs) are frequently used to spell out the terms of collateral arrangements, including the threshold for uncollateralized exposure and acceptable collateral instruments (normally cash and developed-country sovereign and agency debt, though some dealers accept equities and corporate debt). At present, three such CSAs are in use (corresponding to English, Japanese, and U.S. law). ISDA plans to consolidate these into a single core document that addresses the operational and economic aspects, with annexes that cover purely legal aspects.

Operational Risks

The complexity of OTC derivatives contracts gives rise to operational risks, including the aforementioned clearing and settlement risks and a variety of others.[45] Models of derivatives prices may be misspecified, may be miscoded in management information systems, or may break down unexpectedly; this is model risk. The relationship of the price of the derivative to the underlying security and to related hedging instruments can be quite complicated, and major dealers employ teams of highly skilled quantitative analysts to study and manage these relationships. Nonetheless, even sophisticated institutions and well-developed and liquid markets are subject to model risk. For example, the relationships among sterling interest-rate swaps, interest-rate options, and swaptions broke down in 1999, owing to structural developments that the models did not capture.[46]

---

[40]If the option still has some time to go before it expires, it will be worth a bit more than $200. Part of an option's value derives from the fact that one can wait to exercise it.

[41]Greater sensitivity to credit risk at the longer end of the maturity spectrum may also be reflected in wider swap spreads for longer-dated swaps (Kolb (1996), pp. 146–47).

[42]See International Swaps and Derivatives Association, Inc. (1999), p. 2.

[43]In 1993, about half the end-users and all the dealers surveyed by the CFTC reported the use of collateral to manage credit exposures (United States, Commodity Futures Trading Commission, 1993b, p. 77).

[44]United States, General Accounting Office (1999), p. 42, notes that LTCM used rehypothecation to achieve high leverage.

[45]See, for example, Global Derivatives Study Group (1993).

[46]Dunbar (1999).

Box 3.5. Measuring Potential Future Exposure in a Swap Contract

Sharp losses during periods of market turbulence have led to an increased focus on counterparty credit risk in OTC derivatives. This credit risk includes current and potential exposure. Potential future exposure (PFE) is the maximum, the average, or some percentile (for example, the 95th percentile) of the distribution of exposure that might be attained in the future. This distribution (based on simulated future paths for the price of the underlying asset) is known as an exposure profile.

The exposure profile and PFE depend importantly upon the key characteristics of the underlying cashflows, particularly their maturity. For example, exposure tends to rise with maturity because the potential drift in the price of the underlying security also increases with maturity (the diffusion effect). At the same time, the remaining maturity of the contract, and the number of future payments that might be at risk, decrease with the passage of time (the amortization effect).[1] When the diffusion effect is stronger (typically in the early days of the contract's life), the exposure profile rises with time; when the amortization effect is stronger, the exposure profile falls with time. For contracts where principal is exchanged, the exposure profile usually rises continuously until maturity; for others, such as interest rate swaps, the exposure profile is usually hump-shaped.

A simple example can illustrate the principle of exposure profiles and PFE. Consider a very simple interest rate swap where the holder pays a floating rate and receives a fixed rate of interest (12 percent) once a year on a notional principal of $100 million over 5 years. In practice, calculating the PFE on even this simple swap is complicated, because changes in both the level and shape of the yield curve can give rise to large changes in the value of the swap, and because the yield curve evolves over time in a complicated way. To simplify, suppose that (1) the yield curve is initially flat, and remains flat—short-term and long-term interest rates are always exactly the same; (2) interest rates follow a simple process: they start at 12 percent; thereafter, every year, interest rates either increase by one percentage point, decline by one percentage point, or remain unchanged. The valuation of the swap is then very simple; at each point in time, the floating-rate leg is priced at par, and the fixed-rate leg is priced as if it were a fixed-

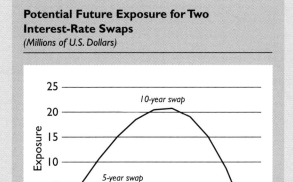

Potential Future Exposure for Two Interest-Rate Swaps
(Millions of U.S. Dollars)

rate bond with a 12 percent coupon. At inception and expiration, the swap is worth zero, since the interest rates on the floating (paying) and fixed (receiving) legs are the same and the cashflows are identical.

The table shows the evolution of interest rates and the value of the swap. If interest rates fall, the value of the swap to the fixed-rate receiver rises (for the same reason that the price of a fixed-rate bond rises), creating credit exposure to the counterparty. If interest rates decline to 11 percent in the first year, for example, the value of the swap to the fixed-rate receiver rises to $3.1 million. If they decline further to 10 percent in the second year, the value of the swap rises further to about $5 million. The maximum exposure is at the lowest level of interest rates that can be attained; the diffusion effect means that interest rates can fall further in years that are farther from inception. As the figure shows, at three years, exposure peaks at about $5.3 million, at which point the amortization effect begins to dominate the diffusion effect. Measuring PFE by maximum exposure, the PFE for the five-year swap is $5.3 million. Comparing a ten-year swap gives a perspective on the importance of maturity (see the second panel of the table). Maximum exposure on the ten-year swap peaks at six years at almost $21 million, about four times the maximum exposure on the five-year swap.

---

[1]See Lau (1997), Chapter 5.

Operational risks are difficult to quantify and manage using tools like the ones used for other risks. In practice, most operational risks are managed by limiting and reserving against exposures that seem vulnerable to operational risks, and by strengthening back-office systems and automating the trade-capture process. As noted above, operational risks associated with the early part of the

trade-capture cycle are viewed as manageable by major market participants. As a result, much of the focus has turned to other operational risks that crop up later—particularly legal risks (see Box 3.6: Legal Risks In OTC Derivatives Markets).[47]

---

[47]See Global Derivatives Study Group (1993).

Potential Exposure Paths for Two $100 Million Notional Fixed-for-Floating Interest Rate Swaps[1]

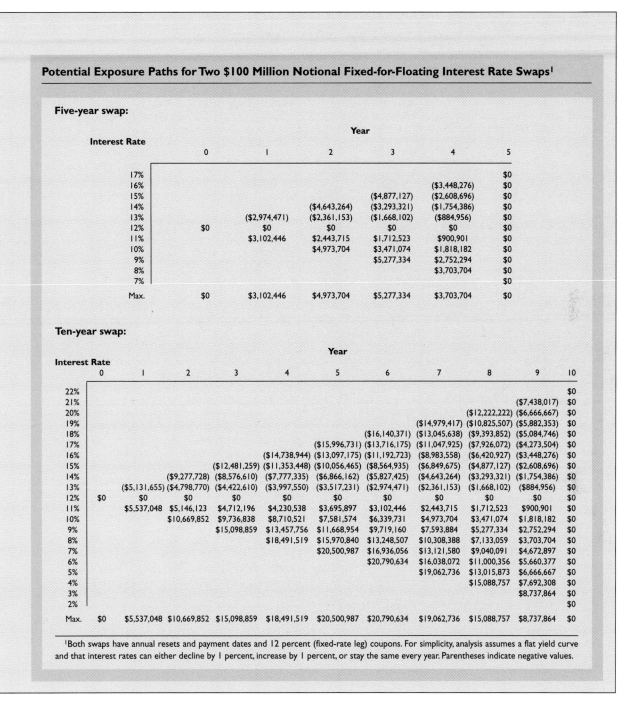

[1]Both swaps have annual resets and payment dates and 12 percent (fixed-rate leg) coupons. For simplicity, analysis assumes a flat yield curve and that interest rates can either decline by 1 percent, increase by 1 percent, or stay the same every year. Parentheses indicate negative values.

The legal risks associated with the use of collateral have been the subject of much recent discussion. Collateral offers substantial protection for swap transactions that are subject to U.S. law since such collateral is specifically recognized in the Financial Institutions Reform Recovery and Enforcement Act of 1989; in addition, swaps counterparties are exempt from the automatic stay provision of the U.S. bankruptcy code.[48] In other segments and jurisdictions, however, collateral can give rise to legal risks at the same time that it alleviates coun-

---

[48]See Wallace (1994). A U.S. bankruptcy bill under consideration in 2000 sought to further clarify the U.S. legal environment for OTC derivatives.

Box 3.6. Legal Risks in OTC Derivatives Markets

OTC derivatives are more lightly regulated than exchange-traded derivatives, so it is not surprising that OTC derivatives transactions have given rise to a number of legal disputes. A recent study found that 76 percent of derivatives cases filed in U.S. federal courts involved OTC derivatives.[1] A number of high-profile cases have illustrated the legal risks in OTC derivatives markets:

Fiduciary Duty in Swap Agreements, and the Legal Environment for Swaps: *Procter & Gamble vs. Bankers Trust* (United States, 1996): This is often viewed as among the first decisions bearing on the OTC derivatives markets, though the judge who ruled made it clear that his decision was meant to apply only to the specific arrangements at hand. Procter & Gamble (P&G) had entered a number of swaps with Bankers Trust (BT), including several highly leveraged swaps linked to interest rates and currencies. In the event, P&G lost some $150 million on the swaps, and claimed (among other things) that: (1) owing to its longstanding relationship with BT, BT owed it a fiduciary duty under these arrangements, and that BT had failed to perform this duty in the context of these swaps; (2) the agreements violated various provisions of, among other things, the Commodity Exchange Act (CEA) and Ohio law. The court ruled that the bilateral, principal-to-principal relationship between P&G and BT did not give rise to a fiduciary duty on BT's part. It also ruled that the swap agreements were exempt from the CEA and that the choice of law provision in the swap agreements (which specified that New York law would govern the agreements) precluded claims under Ohio law.

Ultra Vires: Hazell vs. Hammersmith and Fulham LBC (United Kingdom, 1991). During 1987–89, the local authorities of the London borough of Hammersmith and Fulham entered about 600 swaps and swap derivatives transactions totalling some £6 billion in notional amounts, almost all speculative rather than hedging transactions. After the swaps and swap derivatives went out of the money (by some hundreds of millions of pounds), the authority's auditor asked to have the transactions declared void, claiming that Hammersmith and Fulham did not have the authority to enter them (that is, that the swaps were *ultra vires*). The U.K. court agreed, notwithstanding some prior legal opinions obtained by some counterparties that local authorities did have the power to enter such transactions for risk-management purposes. The decision effectively voided numerous other transactions undertaken by U.K. local authorities, triggering a rash of litigation (however, the court noted that the rights of the authorities and their counterparties to recover payments would have to be determined on a case-by-case basis).

Contract Terms Governing Collateral: *High Risk Opportunities vs. Société Générale SA and Crédit Lyonnais SA* (ongoing). The High-Risk Opportunities Fund (HRO), run by the III Offshore Advisors hedge fund located in West Palm Beach, Florida, made leveraged investments in Russian GKOs and hedged its ruble risk with forwards entered with Société Générale (SG) and Crédit Lyonnais (CL). HRO claimed that, after Russia's devaluation and default on GKOs, SG and CL refused to make margin payments on the forwards, intentionally forcing HRO into bankruptcy. Counsel for SG insisted that the crisis in Russia relieved them of their obligations. As of mid–2000, the case had not yet been concluded.

Definition of "Credit Event:" *Deutsche Bank AG vs. ANZ Banking Group Ltd.,* (1999). A credit default swap between Deutsche Bank and ANZ provided that ANZ would buy City of Moscow bonds from Deutsche Bank if Deutsche Bank notified it that a "credit event" (a "failure to pay" by the City of Moscow) had occurred, based on publicly available information. Deutsche Bank sent ANZ a notice that the City of Moscow had made payments on a loan from Daiwa Bank one day late, providing as evidence an article from *International Financing Review* and noting that the terms of the loan from Daiwa included no grace period. ANZ alleged, among other things, that a credit event had not occurred, because the delay in payment was "technical" rather than "substantial," and moreover claimed that Daiwa had arranged to have the article published in order to collect on payments under one of its own agreements. The court concluded that ANZ was bound to the letter of the agreement and found in favor of Deutsche Bank.

Valuation of Swaps Against a Defaulting Counterparty: *Robinson Department Stores vs. Peregrine Fixed Income* (2000). Robinson Department Stores Plc, a Thai corporation, owed money to Peregrine Fixed Income (PFI) on derivatives transactions it entered before Peregrine's collapse during the Asian crisis. Robinson claimed that the amount it owed should have been reduced because its (Robinson's) creditworthiness has decreased; hence, the value of Peregrine's claim on Robinson had decreased as well. At issue was whether language in ISDA documentation should be interpreted as specifying that the credit standing of the nondefaulting counterparty should be taken into account in valuing terminated swaps. PricewaterhouseCoopers, PFI's liquidator, asked the U.K. court for an interpretation of ISDA documentation in this regard. Some legal experts considered that, if the court found that the amount Robinson owed PFI should be reduced, numerous other ISDA-documented swaps transactions could have been sharply revalued. In May 2000, the U.K. court sided with Peregrine's liquidator; Robinson and other swap creditors will be required to pay in full.

---

[1]PricewaterhouseCoopers, Derivatives Litigation Study (2000) (see website http://www.pwcderivatives. com).

terparty risk. For example, there are important questions about the enforceability of collateral arrangements in some jurisdictions.[49] The legal environment for collateral is particularly murky in cross-border deals. The geographic diversity of counterparties, collateral instruments, and custodial entities gives rise to significant uncertainty about which country's law governs collateral arrangements.[50] At least three sets of law are relevant: the law of the jurisdiction governing the collateral arrangement; the law of the jurisdiction where the collateral is located; and the law of the jurisdiction where the counterparty is located. In addition, procedural slippages such as failing to perfect security interest in overseas collateral are commonplace, leading one legal counsel to suggest that "security of collateral is not widely respected in international finance." Awareness of these issues is improving, and market leaders are making strong efforts to manage the associated risks and ensure that procedures are followed.

Market participants have taken a number of steps to address these operational risks. Considerable effort has been devoted to formalizing and standardizing (or commoditizing) the framework for OTC derivatives transactions, so that traders and back-office personnel correctly document the terms of each trade and both counterparties understand their rights and obligations. The master agreement is a key element of this framework. Various national organizations and business groups, such as the British Bankers Association and ISDA, have promulgated master agreements that are either used verbatim or modified.[51] The most widely used master agreements are the two main ISDA agreements promulgated in 1992: one for transactions in local currency within a single jurisdiction and another for cross-border transactions in multiple currencies.[52] The latter spells out (1) each party's obligations, including making payments as specified in confirmation agreements; (2) repre-

sentations of each party, for example, that it has the power to execute the agreement; (3) agreements that each party will, among other things, supply relevant information to the other and comply with applicable laws; (4) the definition of default or early termination (for example, if changes in law make the agreement illegal, or if relevant taxes change); (5) the right to terminate in case of a termination event; (6) terms for transfer of the agreement to other parties; (7) the currency used for payments; and (8) miscellaneous other provisions, such as the law governing the transaction (commonly English or New York law).[53] Once a master agreement has been put in place between two parties, they may enter OTC derivatives transactions in the context of that agreement (transactions are treated as supplements to the master agreement).

Closeout netting—the settlement of net outstanding obligations by a single payment in the event of default—is a key part of the master agreement, as it limits the risk that the counterparty or trustee will "cherry pick" its obligations. The closeout process can itself be the source of difficulties in stressed markets, however. Under standard agreements, closeout valuations require 4 or 5 market quotes for each contract, and a major derivatives desk may have thousands of contracts with a large counterparty.[54] In addition, the default of Peregrine Fixed Income underlined important unresolved questions about whether counterparty credit risk should be reflected in closeout valuation of swaps.[55] The present industry consensus is that the standard "first" and "second" valuation methods—market quotation and the loss method—do not work well under stress, and that alternatives (such as taking fewer quotes from a wider universe of participants, and lengthening the period of time for obtaining closeout valuations) should be considered.

Legal risks are often reflected in risk management practices. For example, there may be limits on exposures to countries where legal risks are pronounced. If there are concerns that netting may not be enforceable in a particular jurisdiction, or that enforcement may be time-consuming, exposures may be calcu-

---

[49]See Global Derivatives Study Group (1993). For discussion of the legal issues surrounding the use of collateral in Europe, see International Swaps and Derivatives Association (2000).

[50]In the EU, the implementation of the Settlement Finality Directive may clarify these issues ("Collateral Calculations," pp. 44–47).

[51]A recent "master master" cross-product netting agreement permits the netting of counterparty exposures across existing master agreements including for swaps, options, foreign exchange, and repos (see Cass, 2000, p. 17).

[52]German and French counterparties often prefer master agreements written by domestic banking associations to those written by ISDA. The use of different documents for different positions can give rise to "documentation basis risk"; for example, ISDA and Bond Market Association documents might imply different valuations for the same underlying asset (Counterparty Risk Management Policy Group, 1999, p. 42).

[53]Default is distinct from termination. Default indicates a credit problem and entitles the nondefaulting counterparty to terminate all swaps under a master agreement. Termination indicates an event other than a credit problem (say, a change in relevant law) and terminates only those swaps that are directly affected (Marshall and Kapner, 1993, pp. 198–99).

[54]Once these valuations are obtained, the process for making a claim against the counterparty in court is the same as for any other senior claim.

[55]For a description of Peregrine's demise see International Monetary Fund (1998a), Box 2.10, p. 45.

IV Regulatory Environment for OTC Derivatives Activities

Although OTC derivatives on the whole tend to be lightly regulated (as noted in Section III), regulatory systems that are relevant for OTC derivatives can be complex and can have identifiable effects on the organization and location of OTC derivatives activities. Because OTC derivatives transactions usually involve sophisticated counterparties and OTC derivatives markets provide only a limited price discovery function, investor protection and related regulations play only a minor role in the official oversight of the OTC derivatives market. The other two traditional rationales for financial regulation—fostering market efficiency and reducing systemic risk—are important for OTC derivatives markets and are usually addressed by prudential regulations that typically apply to institutions as a whole and not to specific OTC derivatives products. This section illustrates these issues by reviewing the regulatory environments in key jurisdictions. It then analyzes the effects of regulation and regulatory uncertainty on OTC derivatives activities. The section concludes with a discussion of the key challenges for supervision and regulation associated with the use of credit derivatives.

Regulatory Environments in the United States, the United Kingdom, and Other Key Jurisdictions

The United States

The various regulatory agencies in the United States are organized around markets, financial instruments, or institutions, and sometimes span two or three of these concepts.[56] The regulation of financial services has also been tailored according to whether these services are privately or publicly offered, and by whom; whether they are concluded on a principal or agent basis, and on or off an exchange; and whether they involve the commitment of funds to a custodian for investment or safekeeping.

As a result, no single U.S. regulator governs the many types of derivatives products traded in the OTC market. Derivatives range from products that are subject to comprehensive futures or securities regulations—mostly instruments traded on organized exchanges subject to rules on price transparency, trade practices, and anti-manipulation protections—to historically unregulated transactions such as forward contracts. Further complicating the regulatory environment is the fact that OTC derivatives are used by entities that are subject to one or more regulatory regimes, either as intermediaries (for example, securities broker-dealers, and futures commission merchants) or as end-users (such as pension funds and investment companies).

There are three key financial regulators whose mandates impinge directly on OTC derivatives activities: the Commodity Futures Trading Commission (CFTC); the Securities and Exchange Commission (SEC); and bank regulators. The CFTC oversees organized derivatives exchanges (primarily futures markets) and transactions in futures contracts and commodity options. It also supervises intermediaries that operate in these markets, such as futures commission merchants (FCMs). The CFTC imposes minimum capital requirements on FCMs and requires FCMs to have adequate internal controls, record keeping, and reporting procedures. CFTC rules also preclude certain types of end-users (primarily small private customers) from engaging in various OTC derivatives transactions.

The Commodity Exchange Act (CEA) is the legal basis for the CFTC's authority. Under the CEA, futures contracts and commodity options have to be traded exclusively on CFTC-approved exchanges, unless there are specific exemptions. Forward contracts have traditionally been expressly excluded from the CEA and are thus unregulated. The CFTC's rules applicable to OTC derivatives have evolved as a series of exceptions to the CEA, its exchange-trading re-

---

[56]For an overview of the regulatory environment in the United States see, for example, United States, Commodity Futures Trading Commission (1993a); and particularly the associated working papers 3A, 3B, and 3C, which cover the regulatory frameworks for the CFTC, the SEC, and bank regulators, respectively.

quirement, and other regulatory requirements. In 1993, the CFTC exempted swap agreements from most provisions of the CEA, subject to restrictions on the design and execution of such transactions. The exemption criteria, which were meant to prevent an unregulated exchange-like market in swaps, have created a significant degree of ambiguity and uncertainty about the regulatory treatment of swaps, as financial and technical innovations (such as electronic trading and settlement) have tested the limits of the swaps exemption (which is explained further, below).

The SEC enforces federal securities laws that cover transactions in "securities" as defined by law, including some OTC derivatives such as securities options.[57] The SEC oversees both primary and secondary markets in securities, and also regulates securities broker-dealers.[58] A key issue in determining whether the SEC regulates derivatives—and financial institutions trading them—is the extent to which such derivatives are "securities" in the legal definition, or are embedded in instruments that are predominantly securities. For example, options on securities, securities indices, and certificates of deposit that are not traded on exchanges are considered securities and are thus subject to SEC regulation. Securities derivatives are subject to the SEC's entire regulatory framework, regardless of whether these products are traded on registered exchanges or in the OTC market. To the extent that OTC market participants and market makers for OTC options act as brokers[59] or as dealers[60] in securities, they are subject to the SEC's extensive regulatory requirements applicable to broker-dealers, including capital and margin requirements.

Because a growing market share of the activities in OTC derivatives contracts that are not considered securities is conducted by unregistered affiliates of registered broker-dealers, the SEC adopted in 1992 a "Risk Assessment Program" to monitor the risks such activities pose for parent broker-dealers. Members of the Derivatives Policy Group (DPG), which include the largest broker-dealers and FCMs, voluntarily disclose information about their unregistered affiliates whose activities may have a material impact on the parent broker-dealers and FCMs.[61] As part of this program, the SEC and the CFTC receive quarterly information on derivatives positions, internal controls, and risk management techniques.

Banks are supervised by the Office of the Comptroller of the Currency, the Federal Deposit Insurance Corporation, the Federal Reserve, or by state banking regulators, depending on the type of their bank charter, deposit insurance, and Federal Reserve membership. In contrast to futures and securities regulators, banking regulators approach financial activities almost exclusively from the point of view of the integrity of the individual institution and its capacity to perform banking functions. Banking supervision therefore only involves direct oversight of institutions and does not rely on oversight of markets or specific financial products. Bank supervisors can address derivatives activities by limiting the types of permissible transactions, imposing internal control and risk management requirements, and by requiring that appropriate levels of capital are held against derivatives positions.

Wholesale Market Regime in the United Kingdom

The U.K. context has two important features: first, a single financial regulator, the Financial Services Authority (FSA), is being established, and second, U.K. regulators differentiate the regulatory treatment of professional and nonprofessional business according to the market participants' degree of experience and expertise, and their relative need for protection. As in many other countries, there is no system of product regulations in the United Kingdom, but there are conduct of business re-

---

[57]According to the 1934 Securities Exchange Act, the legal definition of a "security" is: "any note, stock, treasury stock, bond debenture, certificate of interest or participation in any profit-sharing agreement or in any oil, gas, or other mineral royalty or lease, any collateral-trust certificate, preorganization certificate or subscription, transferable share, investment contract, voting-trust certificate, certificate of deposit, for a security, any put, call, straddle, option or privilege on any security, certificate of deposit, or group or index of securities (including any interest therein or based on the value thereof) or any put, call, straddle, option or privilege entered into on a national securities exchange relating to foreign currency, or in general, any instrument commonly known as a "security"; or any certificate of interest or participation in, temporary or interim certificate for, receipt for, or warrant or right to subscribe to or purchase, any of the foregoing . . . ." [1932 Act § 3(a), 15 U.S.C. §78c(a) (10)].

[58]In addition to exchange regulation, the SEC framework includes regulation of primary public offerings of securities (product registration and disclosure requirements). This is in contrast to futures regulations, where the main focus rests on transactions in the secondary exchange market since all futures transactions are required to be effected on a centralized exchange without an offering process comparable to that of securities.

[59]A "broker" is defined in the 1934 Securities Exchange Act (SEA) as "any person engaged in the business of effecting transactions in securities for the account of others, but not a bank."

[60]A "dealer" is defined in the SEA as "any person engaged in the business of buying and selling securities for his own account,

---

through a broker or otherwise, but does not include a bank, or any person insofar as he buys or sells securities for his own account, either individually or in some fiduciary capacity, but not as a part of a regular business."

[61]For more information on DPG, see United States General Accounting Office (1999), pp. 17 and 27.

quirements that normally apply to all "investment" transactions.[62]

A special wholesale market regime (the Grey Paper Regime) applies to clearly defined wholesale transactions and provides "light touch" supervision and regulation.[63] Within this special market regime, fewer requirements apply to listed "wholesale money market institutions," which comprise both banks and securities houses. Certain activities of listed institutions are exempt from the Financial Services Act. They include dealing in investments, arranging deals in investments, and advising on investments. The rationale for the FSA's "Grey Paper Regime" for the wholesale cash and OTC derivatives markets is that "caveat emptor" should be applied to dealings between firms and their professional counterparties to a larger extent than to dealings with retail customers.[64, 65]

The relevant wholesale markets are defined by the products traded in them, the institutions conducting the trading, and minimum size of transactions.[66] Central to the regulatory regime is a list of institutions that act in the relevant markets either as principal or broker.[67] An applicant needs to demonstrate to the FSA that it is financially sound and has an appropriate ownership structure, managerial and operational resources, and that its systems and controls are adequate. The FSA does not list institutions as wholesale money market institutions that are generally regarded as customers or end-users.

The core of the wholesale market regime is a prescribed code of business conduct (the "London Code") that wholesale market institutions must comply with.[68] The London Code has been developed in close cooperation with market participants and sets out principles, standards, and controls that participants in the wholesale market should observe. It applies to most wholesale market dealings that are not regulated by the rules of a recognized exchange. The Code comprises general standards (which describe the responsibilities of principals, brokers, and employees), principles of control (including know-your-counterparty and confidentiality rules), and best practices for dealing procedures.

Unlike in the United States, legislation in the United Kingdom permits "recognized clearing-houses" for OTC markets that are supervised by the FSA on criteria set out in the Financial Services Act. Similarly, multilateral trading of OTC derivatives products is, in principle, permitted. Any person offering multilateral execution facilities would, however, be regarded as conducting investment business and would therefore require authorization. Persons offering multilateral trading facilities for OTC derivatives that do not fall within the definition of "investment" would not be subject to the requirements of the Financial Services Act. For example, the Exchange Clearing House (ECHO) provides netting facilities for spot and forward foreign exchange contracts that are not considered investments. ECHO is nevertheless listed as a money market institution and is therefore supervised by the FSA.

Regulatory and Supervisory Frameworks in Other Financial Jurisdictions

Regulations and supervision relevant for OTC derivatives markets typically have five dimensions: permitted transactions; authorization and licensing of counterparties; restrictions on counterparties; rules for market making and trading; and disclosure requirements.[69]

Most jurisdictions do not impose restrictions on the design of OTC derivatives products and thus do not limit the range of products that can be traded. Particularly, nonstandardized bilateral OTC transactions between licensed counterparties or banks are typically not directly regulated. Although OTC transactions are mostly not regulated through market- or product-based requirements, they are indirectly affected by prudential and conduct regulations that are aimed at financial institutions.

---

[62]See United States, Commodity Futures Trading Commission (1999).

[63]See United Kingdom, Financial Services Authority (1999b).

[64]The Securities and Futures Authority (SFA), which is now integrated into the FSA, had a similar differentiation in its rulebook. But the two approaches differ in terms of the criteria for eligibility: while the Grey Paper is essentially transactions-based, the SFA's approach is counterparty-based.

[65]The wholesale market regime is currently being revised in light of the new Financial Services and Markets Bill, which will formally establish the FSA as the single financial regulator in the U.K. The new "inter-professional regime" would combine the FSA's Grey Paper Regime with the SFA's approach to professional business. It will likely be extended to a wider range of OTC products, notably equity, commodity, and energy derivatives, and may distinguish three tiers of market participants—market counterparties, intermediate customers, and private customers—rather than the two-way split between professional and nonprofessional counterparties under the current regime.

[66]The minimum size limits are (£100,000 for debentures, bonds, loan stock, and sale and repurchase agreements; and an underlying notional value of (£500,000 for swaps, options, futures, and forward rate agreements or any other "contract for differences" (see United Kingdom, Financial Services Authority, 1999b).

[67]Under EU directives, a bank or nonbank investment firm incorporated and authorized in another EU Member Country may conduct the range of investment services in the United Kingdom. It is authorized by its home country regulator; further U.K. authorization is not required.

[68]See United Kingdom, Financial Services Authority (1999a).

[69]For a comprehensive overview of OTC derivatives regulations in key jurisdictions, see United States, Commodity Futures Trading Commission (1999).

In most countries, authorization rules for participants in the OTC derivatives market generally differ depending on whether the institutions are conducting business exclusively on their own account or engage in transactions on behalf of clients. Most countries do not have licensing requirements specifically for OTC counterparties. An important exception is Japan, where securities firms need special authorization to engage in OTC derivatives. In Europe, by contrast, if a party to an OTC derivatives transaction effects the transaction for proprietary purposes, it does not need a license. However, if a firm undertakes OTC derivative transactions on behalf of customers, it must be licensed as a financial services or credit institution and is then subject to standard supervision since, according to the EU Investment Services Directive, OTC financial derivatives activities are considered investment business. If authorization is required, it is up to the home country supervisor to decide whether or not to license an institution for the full range of financial services or whether to restrict the authorization to conduct OTC business based on an assessment of whether the firm is fit and proper. Some European countries restrict the use of OTC derivatives by collective investment schemes (including France and Spain). Germany, in addition, restricts the use of OTC derivatives by insurance companies and mortgage banks.

Only in very few jurisdictions are OTC derivatives transactions prohibited outright for particular types of counterparties (such as retail end-users), but some countries have "suitability" rules that determine what types of transactions are suitable for a given counterparty. A case in point is Australia, where unsophisticated counterparties are not allowed to trade on OTC derivatives markets (under Australia's exempt futures declaration) and thus must use exchange markets. Most countries do not prohibit individuals from engaging in OTC derivatives transactions, but some jurisdictions impose additional requirements on transactions with retail or unsophisticated customers and lower requirements for wholesale or professional market participants. Many countries require that dealers transacting with non-dealers in derivatives markets obtain information about their customers to help ensure the customer's suitability.[70] In some cases (for example, in

Germany) special disclosures are required when dealing with unsophisticated counterparties.

A few jurisdictions have rules that restrict market making, multilateral trading, or centralized clearing of OTC derivatives transactions. Similar to the case in the United States, in Australia, exempt futures markets (that is, OTC derivatives markets) are prohibited from having centralized clearing systems and multilateral trading facilities. But most countries have no explicit rules against multilateral electronic execution facilities, and a number of jurisdictions explicitly permit centralized clearing of OTC derivatives, including the United Kingdom, Sweden, and the Netherlands. Choice of law provisions (which are important since ISDA master agreements are drafted only for New York and English law) are accepted in most jurisdictions, though some uncertainty remains about their enforceability in court.

Effects of Regulatory Rules and Modes of Supervision on the OTC Derivatives Markets

Despite the fact that OTC derivatives are one of the least regulated segments of financial markets, their flexibility and global reach facilitates regulatory arbitrage so that even relatively "light touch" regulation and supervision have identifiable effects on the OTC derivatives markets. This is particularly apparent in the organization of the market, the way in which products are traded and transactions cleared, and the location of specific OTC derivatives transactions. These decisions, and thus indirectly the regulatory framework, have implications for the distribution of risks in the OTC derivatives markets, and for the effectiveness of market surveillance.

A key question for a U.S. nonbank financial institution is whether an OTC derivative transaction must be booked in a registered (and thus regulated) broker-dealer or can be done through an unregulated affiliate.[71] If the OTC derivative instrument is a "security" as defined by law, the transaction has to be conducted through a registered broker-dealer, which is subject to the Securities Exchange Act and supervised by the SEC. The term "security" includes stocks and bonds, but also options on securities and indices of securities. Thus, while some OTC derivatives instruments are considered securities (such as OTC options on equities and U.S. government securities), others are not (swaps, for example).

The potential costs associated with broker-dealer regulation in the United States (compliance with

---

[70]A joint statement on oversight of the OTC derivatives market (March 15, 1994) by the U.S. CFTC, U.S. SEC, and the U.K. Securities and Investment Board (SIB) (which is now part of the FSA) states: "Having regard to the complexity and lack of transparency characteristic for many OTC derivatives products, the Authorities, as necessary, will encourage the development of a regulatory framework that addresses the particular suitability, know your customer or access issues arising in OTC derivatives transactions." See United States, Commodity Futures Trading Commission (1999), p. 57.

[71]These considerations do not apply to banks, which are regulated and supervised by the relevant U.S. banking regulator.

capital requirements, disclosure rules, and margin requirements) have affected the way U.S. securities firms conduct their OTC derivative transactions.[72] Since those derivative transactions that are considered securities in the United States (such as equity derivatives) would fall under SEC jurisdiction, these transactions are mostly conducted abroad through American broker-dealer affiliates located primarily in London. For those transactions that are not securities, most broker-dealers have established unregulated affiliates within the United States. Unregulated affiliates, which have grown rapidly in recent years, often hold large OTC derivatives positions and can be major providers of credit (and therefore leverage) to market participants, including to hedge funds.[73] Such affiliates avoid the explicit and implicit costs of regulation, but add to the operational complexity of the parent firm and contribute to legal, operational, and other risks. According to some market participants, multiple legal entities also limit the use of some risk mitigation techniques, such as netting, and complicate interactions with customers.

Unregulated affiliates can also pose challenges for supervision and market surveillance since these affiliates are not subject to reporting requirements.[74] But information on unregulated affiliates is not completely lacking. As mentioned above, since 1994, the six largest U.S. securities broker-dealers and futures commission merchants, which form the DPG, have agreed to provide the SEC and the CFTC with information about risk profiles, credit quality and credit concentrations, and the quality of internal controls of their affiliates that deal in OTC derivatives.

To further improve market surveillance, consideration has been given to integrate unregulated broker-dealer affiliates—to varying degrees—into official oversight. A special voluntary regulatory regime for OTC derivatives dealers that offers lighter regulation and supervision than for registered broker-dealers has been introduced by the SEC. More recently, two alternative approaches have been advanced: special reporting requirements, and outright regulation of OTC affiliates.

To integrate activities of unregulated affiliates into official oversight, the SEC has established the category of "OTC Derivatives Dealers" (see Box 4.1: SEC-Registered "OTC Derivatives Dealers").[75] Securities firms can—on a voluntary basis—establish separately capitalized entities that deal in eligible OTC derivatives instruments, including both securities and nonsecurities OTC derivatives instruments. These entities would face a less burdensome regulatory capital regime than traditional broker-dealers, but would be subject to reporting requirements and oversight of their internal control systems. This special "broker-dealer lite" approach was also designed to allow U.S. broker-dealers to compete more effectively and to conduct more efficient risk management by centralizing both securities and nonsecurities OTC derivatives transactions in one legal entity. However, it is doubtful whether many broker-dealers will voluntarily register their affiliates as "OTC Derivatives Dealers," since broker-dealers can continue to achieve even more regulatory relief through unregulated affiliates—admittedly with the drawback that unregulated affiliates cannot offer the complete line of OTC derivatives.

As for reporting requirements, the President's Working Group on Financial Markets (PWG)[76] recommended expanding the authority of regulators to require broker-dealers, futures commission merchants, and their unregulated affiliates to report information on credit risks, exposure concentrations, trading strategies, and risk models.[77] A report by the General Accounting Office proposed that Congress consider expanding the SEC's and CFTC's regulatory authority to examine unregistered affiliates of broker-dealers and FCMs, set capital standards, and take enforcement actions, with a view to more effective oversight of potential systemic risks in financial markets.[78]

---

[72]Registered broker-dealers have to comply with the SEC's net capital rule which requires, for example, that swaps have to be covered by 100 percent net capital on the replacement value. In fact, this capital requirement on swaps for broker-dealers is larger than the requirement for banks, which according to the Basel Capital Accord have to hold a capital charge of at most 8 percent of the replacement value (depending on the type of counterparty)—plus a small charge to capture potential future exposure. The President's Working Group on Financial Markets advised the SEC to explore more risk-sensitive approaches to capital for securities firms, building on the experience with the "broker-dealer lite" approach to capital for derivatives dealers (see below). See United States, President's Working Group on Financial Markets (1999a) and United States, Securities and Exchange Commission (1997).

[73]At four major securities and futures firms, the share of assets held outside regulated entities rose from 22 percent in 1994 to 41 percent in 1998, according to the U.S. General Accounting Office (see United States, General Accounting Office (1999)).

[74]See United States, General Accounting Office (1999); and United States, President's Working Group on Financial Markets (1999a).

[75]See United States, Securities and Exchange Commission (1999).

[76]The U.S. President's Working Group on Financial Markets consists of senior representatives from the Department of the Treasury, the Federal Reserve Board, the Securities and Exchange Commission, and the Commodity Futures Commission.

[77]See United States, President's Working Group on Financial Markets (1999a).

[78]See United States, General Accounting Office (1999).

Box 4.1. SEC-Registered "OTC Derivatives Dealers"[1]

A SEC-registered "OTC Derivatives Dealer" must be affiliated with a fully regulated broker-dealer. At the same time, however, the parent broker-dealer is prevented from moving its general securities business into the OTC derivatives dealer or from using the affiliate for extensive proprietary trading. Eligible OTC derivatives instruments include both securities and nonsecurities OTC derivatives instruments; securities derivatives that are listed or traded on a national securities exchange or on NASDAQ are excluded. "OTC Derivatives Dealers" must comply with reporting requirements and must establish comprehensive systems of internal controls for managing risks.

As key advantages, "OTC Derivatives Dealers" are exempted from certain provisions of the Securities Exchange Act and the Securities Investor Protection Act, and they face reduced capital requirements and margin rules. A special net capital rule allows OTC dealers to use value-at-risk models to calculate capital charges for market risk (subject to SEC approval) and to take lower charges for credit risk than broker-dealers. The credit risk capital charge consists of two parts: (1) similar to the Basel Accord charge for banks, a capital charge that depends on the creditworthiness of the counterparty and is based on the net replacement value of all outstanding transactions with each counterparty, taking netting and collateral arrangements into account; and (2) a special charge if the net replacement value of positions with any single counterparty exceeds 25 percent of the OTC dealer's net capital. "OTC Derivatives Dealers" that extend credit have to comply with the less onerous Regulation U on margin requirements (which applies to banks) rather than the stricter Regulation T (which applies to broker-dealers).

---

[1]For a complete description of the regulations that apply to SEC-registered OTC Derivatives Dealers, see United States, Securities and Exchange Commission (1999).

Regulatory Uncertainties and Their Implications for OTC Derivatives

Conceptually, the regulatory treatment of many OTC derivatives lies somewhere between full regulation and (almost) no regulation. As financial products evolve and technology introduces new structures for trading and clearing, these regulatory boundaries are being tested. Associated uncertainties about the applicability of regulations influence activities in the OTC derivatives market. Particularly in such a dynamic and relatively unstructured area as OTC derivatives, legal certainty is crucial. Counterparties must be certain that the contracts they enter into are permissible in the given jurisdiction and that the provisions of the contracts are enforceable. Any hint of legal ambiguities could impede innovation and move trading to jurisdictions that provide firmer grounds. This is, to some extent, the case in the United States, where financial innovation may have been stymied by "[a] cloud of legal uncertainty [that] has hung over the OTC derivatives market in the United States."[79]

In the United States, legal uncertainties arise primarily from three sources. First, there are concerns about whether some OTC swap contracts (primarily those that are standardized, which compose the bulk of swaps) could be construed to be futures contracts and would thus be subject to the CEA. Second, there are questions about whether certain types of mechanisms for executing and clearing of OTC derivatives could alter the status of otherwise exempted or excluded instruments. Finally, there are also ambiguities about which securities-based derivatives fall under the jurisdiction of the SEC or CFTC, or may in fact be prohibited. These uncertainties force financial institutions to carefully evaluate legal risks when they develop new products and, as a result, may have reduced the flexibility of financial markets.

Uncertainties about the standing of swap agreements have emerged in connection with the CFTC's Swap Exemption. The Futures Trading Practices Act of 1992 granted the CFTC authority to exempt certain transactions from the CEA (and from exchange trading requirements). The CFTC has used this authority to exempt swap agreements, hybrid instruments, and certain OTC energy contracts. Exemptions of these instruments from the CEA were deemed justified since prices established in these OTC derivatives markets do not serve a significant price discovery function and are less susceptible to manipulation than prices established in regulated futures markets.

In 1993, the CFTC issued the Swap Exemption, which excludes any swap agreement from the CEA that meets certain criteria. These criteria impose restrictions on the design and execution of transactions that distinguish the exempted swap transactions from exchange-traded products, and are meant to prevent the emergence of an unregulated exchange-like market for swaps. To qualify for the exemption,

---

[79]See United States, President's Working Group on Financial Markets (1999b), page 1 of the transmittal letters.

a swap must be concluded between eligible swap participants; cannot be standardized as to the material economic terms; cannot be part of a central clearing arrangement; and cannot be traded through a multilateral transaction execution facility (MTEF).[80]

Uncertainties in the interpretation of these conditions have, however, emerged. The rise of electronic trading has blurred the line between bilateral and multilateral trading, and the advantage of centralized clearing systems has become widely recognized as trading volumes have increased and a wider range of users have entered the market.[81] As a result, the limits of the swap exemption have become viewed as impediments to further developing the swaps market and in particular seem to be inhibiting the industry's consideration of introducing electronic trading platforms and clearing arrangements to mitigate risks.

In response, the PWG called for a clarification of the swap exemption, the admissibility of clearing arrangements, and a review of the regulatory status of electronic trading systems for swaps.[82] The PWG did not see compelling evidence that would warrant regulation of swaps:[83] most swaps dealers are affiliated with broker-dealers (which are supervised by the SEC), with FCMs (which are supervised by the CFTC), or with banks (which are subject to supervision by bank regulators); and OTC derivatives markets do not serve a significant price discovery function. The Working Group therefore recommended that the exclusion of swaps should be codified as statute by Congress.[84] Under this recommendation, bilateral swap agreements entered into by eligible swap participants on a principal-to-principal basis should, in principle, be excluded from the CEA.[85] The PWG also recommended that electronic multilateral trading systems where participants act solely for their own account should be excluded from CEA regulation since they have the potential to promote efficiency, transparency, and liquidity, and to reduce risks. According to the PWG, the method by which a transaction is executed has no obvious bearing on the need for regulation in markets that are not used for price discovery. Exchanges that have been desig-

nated as contract markets by the CFTC should also be permitted to establish electronic multilateral trading systems for qualified swaps.

Standardization and clearing of exempted swaps should also be permitted, subject to appropriate regulatory oversight, since central clearing can reduce counterparty risks by mutualizing risks, and by facilitating offsets and netting (see Box 4.2: Clearinghouses). While recognizing that clearing tends to concentrate risks and responsibilities for risk management in a central clearinghouse, the PWG recommended that organizations that clear futures, commodity options, and options on futures should be authorized to clear OTC derivatives, subject to CFTC oversight. Similarly, securities clearinghouses, which are subject to SEC oversight, should be authorized to clear OTC derivatives. Clearing through foreign clearing systems should be allowed if these systems are supervised by foreign financial regulators according to standards.

Regulatory uncertainties have restricted the type of underlying securities for OTC derivatives.[86] Ambiguities about the extent of CFTC or SEC jurisdiction to regulate certain securities-based derivatives, such as equity swaps, credit swaps, and emerging country debt swaps, are largely the legacy of the 1974 amendment of the CEA that gave the CFTC exclusive jurisdiction over all futures (on physical and financial commodities) without superseding or limiting the jurisdiction of the SEC.[87] But the broad definition of "commodity" in the Commodity Exchange Act raised concerns that OTC markets for government securities and foreign currency would have been covered by the Act.[88] Therefore—upon the Treasury's request—an amendment (the Treasury Amendment of 1974) was inserted into the Act that excluded from it, among other things, transactions in foreign currency, government securities, and mortgages, "unless such transactions involve the

---

[80]For a detailed list of these swap conditions, see United States, President's Working Group on Financial Markets (1999b).

[81]See Folkerts-Landau and Steinherr (1994) and United States, President's Working Group on Financial Markets (1999b).

[82]See United States, President's Working Group on Financial Markets (1999b).

[83]See Summers (2000).

[84]Several draft bills addressing the swap exclusion are currently being debated in House and Senate committees.

[85]These derivative transactions should also be excluded from certain state laws (for example, gambling laws). The exclusion should, however, not apply to any swap agreement that involves a nonfinancial commodity with finite supply owing to concerns about possible market manipulation.

[86]Innovation in securities-based derivatives, such as equity swaps, credit swaps, and emerging country debt swaps, may have been slowed by ambiguity about supervisory authority in the U.S. and by concerns about their legal enforceability. In fact, Federal Reserve Chairman Greenspan noted that "[t]he greatest legal uncertainty is in the area of securities-based [OTC derivative] contracts, where the CFTC's authority is constrained." See Greenspan (2000).

[87]Specifically, the CFTC was given exclusive jurisdiction over contracts for the sale of a commodity for future delivery and over options on such contracts. It also regulates, though not necessarily with exclusive jurisdiction, commodity option contracts. Transactions in, or in connection with, commodity futures contracts and commodity options must be conducted in accordance with the CEA.

[88]The CEA defines "commodity" as to include agricultural commodities and "all other goods, ... and all services, rights, and interests in which contracts for future delivery are presently or in the future dealt in."

Box 4.2. Clearinghouses

Some have suggested that an exchange-style clearinghouse for OTC derivatives that served as central counterparty could simplify risk management, confirm trades, and net exposures multilaterally, resulting in lower counterparty, operational, legal, and liquidity risks.[1] A clearinghouse for OTC derivatives might increase the scope for early unwinding of contracts and improve the liquidity of OTC derivatives markets through offset (extinguishing a position by taking an opposite position).[2] At present, relatively few OTC derivatives contracts are terminated or transferred (assigned) before they expire, in part because termination may have undesirable tax consequences, and ordinarily both counterparties must agree to an assignment. More often, exposures are unwound by entering an opposite contract. Without offset—for example, cancellation of the original obligation by entering an opposite obligation—an opposite obligation may reduce market risk, but at the cost of increasing counterparty risk.

A few clearing arrangements are already in place, though they probably handle only a tiny amount of global OTC activity. In Sweden, the OM Exchange clears, sets margins, and performs multilateral netting on OTC contracts. In November 1999, the Eurex exchange announced plans to offer clearing of OTC Euri-bor deals (initially Eurex members could use the Eurex clearinghouse to clear OTC trades in short-term Euribor futures). Also, in August 1999, the London Clearing House (LCH) set up the SwapClear facility to clear "vanilla" interest-rate swaps and FRAs of ten years' maturity or less denominated in dollars, euros, pounds sterling, or yen (the system has received an exemption from CFTC regulation; the LCH also has an arrangement for the clearing of repo transactions, called RepoClear). Margin requirements and contingencies in the event of member default are similar to those for exchange-traded contracts. Only a few banks initially participated in SwapClear, though more were expected to join later.

Major dealers are generally wary of centralized clearing arrangements. Some have raised questions about how the multilateral clearing of selected contracts would affect bilateral and multiproduct netting agreements. Others have pointed out that clearinghouses might be tainted by adverse selection, as lower-rated banks would find such an arrangement more attractive than highly rated banks would; others have raised concerns about moral hazard. Still others have concerns that only a limited array of swaps will be eligible for clearing, and that liquidity may become fragmented between SwapClear and the overall OTC market. Key players may also be opposed to a clearinghouse for strategic business reasons, as clearinghouses would lower the "cost of admission" to OTC derivatives markets by mitigating counterparty risk. The assessment and management of counterparty risks is a key source of value added to major market players, who do not want additional competition amid narrowing bid-ask spreads. Finally (as explained above), some aspects of the U.S. regulatory regime have raised concerns that centrally cleared contracts may be regulated as exchange-traded contracts.

---

[1]See Folkerts-Landau and Steinherr (1994). The effect that the introduction of a clearinghouse would have on the nature and distribution of risks in OTC derivatives markets would depend in part upon the structure of the clearinghouse. Principal clearinghouses act as principals to trades, and assume the counterparty risk of clearing members; fiduciary clearinghouses execute members' instructions and safeguard their assets in an agency capacity, and do not assume counterparty risk on cleared transactions.

[2]See Hills, Rule, Parkinson, and Young (1999).

---

sale thereof for future delivery conducted on a board of trade." However, these amendments did not eliminate conflicts regarding each agency's jurisdiction. Ambiguities and potential overlaps of CFTC and SEC jurisdictions remained, in particular, over novel financial instruments that have elements of securities and futures or commodity option contracts. In an attempt to address these problems, the Shad-Johnson Accord between the SEC and the CFTC was concluded in 1983, which explicitly prohibits futures contracts based on the value of an individual security (other than certain "exempt securities").[89] The

Accord also gives the SEC authority over options on securities, certificates of deposit, foreign currencies traded on a national securities exchange, and groups of indices of securities. The CFTC obtained authority over futures contracts and options on futures contracts on exempt securities, certificates of deposit, and indices of securities. The Shad-Johnson Accord, however, itself created some uncertainty, particularly about the status of swap agreements that reference "nonexempt securities," such as equity swaps, credit swaps, and emerging market debt swaps. From time to time, concerns arose that these swaps might be viewed by regulators as futures contracts on nonexempt securities, which in fact would be prohibited by the Shad-Johnson Accord.

To eliminate these ambiguities, the PWG recommended to alter the Treasury Amendment to pre-

---

[89]"Exempt securities" include government securities and other securities that are exempt from many of the federal securities laws.

serve the CFTC's authority to regulate transactions in Treasury Amendment instruments only to the extent that these transactions occur on an exchange that is open to retail or agency transactions.[90] Other markets for Treasury Amendment securities would be explicitly excluded from the CEA. There would also be scope for electronic trading of such instruments outside of the CEA, and, as in the case of exempted swaps, clearing of Treasury Amendment instruments, subject to official oversight, would be allowed without affecting their exclusion from the CEA. The Working Group also recommended to explicitly exclude hybrid instruments that reference securities from the Shad-Johnson Accord.[91]

Financial Innovations and Challenges for Supervision and Regulation: The Case of Credit Derivatives

Credit derivatives are one of the fastest growing areas of the OTC derivatives market. Credit derivatives, however, can be a source of regulatory ambiguities. Since they combine features of traditional credit products and features of traded instruments, they are difficult to integrate into existing regulatory and supervisory frameworks, and they challenge the way bank supervisors have traditionally viewed credit risk: as a cradle-to-grave phenomenon where banks hold credit exposures until maturity and only get actively involved in managing credit risk in the workout of problem loans.[92] With the use of credit derivatives, by contrast, banks can actively unbundle and manage credit risks in novel ways, and can alter their credit risk profiles rapidly.

What distinguishes credit derivatives from many other OTC derivatives is that credit derivatives give rise to dual credit exposures: a credit exposure to a counterparty (as in other OTC derivatives) and a credit exposure to the reference asset.[93] Notwith-

standing this duality, there are no uniform global standards that specify whether a credit derivative position should be viewed as being primarily part of the banking book (which would stress the credit risk in the reference asset) or the trading book (which would stress the credit risk of the counterparty).

Within the Basel Accord on capital adequacy for banks, capital treatments of credit derivatives differ depending on whether the credit risk of the reference asset or the counterparty credit risk is viewed as the primary risk in the credit derivatives position. In the latter case (the derivatives approach), credit derivatives are viewed just as other derivatives, such as interest rate swaps, and the capital requirements are mostly based on the market value of the derivatives position. By contrast, the direct credit substitute approach treats credit derivatives as similar to traditional credit instruments, such as letters of credit and guarantees, and capital charges are based on the total nominal value (notional value of the derivatives position). As a result, capital charges based on the direct credit substitute approach (in the banking book) tend to be much larger than the charge according to the derivatives approach (in the trading book). Thus a bank can "leverage" its credit exposures significantly more by investing in credit derivatives that are part of its trading book than by funding loans.

To illustrate, consider the example of a total rate of return swap (TRORS). If the TRORS is treated as a credit substitute, the guarantor would have to hold 8 percent capital toward the nominal amount of the guarantee (the notional value of the derivative) if the reference asset is a corporate liability or loan. If, by contrast, the same credit derivative is treated as a standard derivative instrument, the capital charge to cover credit risk would be much lower and would have two components: (1) a charge based on the type of counterparty assessed on the market value of the derivative (8 percent for corporate counterparties, 1.6 percent for a bank counterparty), and (2) a (small) charge to cover potential future exposure that is calculated as a percentage (an "add-on factor") of the notional value. Moreover, the matrix of add-on factors in the Basel Accord does not specify the value of add-on factors for credit derivatives (it only contains add-on factors for interest rate, foreign exchange, equity, and commodity derivatives). National regulators therefore have to issue their own guidelines. For example, the Federal Reserve decided to apply equity add-on factors when the reference asset is an investment-grade instrument (or its bank-internal equivalent) or is unrated but well secured by collateral, and to apply the commodity add-on factors for all other reference assets.[94]

[90]Treasury Amendment securities (which include government securities, mortgages, and foreign currency) and options on foreign currency that trade on securities exchanges would continue to be subject to SEC jurisdiction. See United States, President's Working Group on Financial Markets (1999b).

[91]Parallel to clarifying the legal status of OTC derivatives, the CFTC—with support from the President's Working Group—has been reviewing the regulation of exchange-traded financial derivatives. Key elements of this review include "a move from direct to more oversight regulation; a move from prescriptive rules to flexible performance standards; and the increased use of disclosure-based regulation" (see Rainer (2000)). A CFTC Task Force has issued a paper outlining possible measures to streamline the regulation of futures markets (see United States, Commodity Futures Trading Commission Staff Task Force (2000)).

[92]See Staehle and Cumming (1998).

[93]For a more extensive discussion of supervisory and regulatory aspects of credit derivatives, see Staehle and Cumming (1998).

[94]See United States, Board of Governors of the Federal Reserve System (1997).

V Key Features of OTC Derivatives Activities

Against the structural and institutional background laid out in the previous sections, it is useful to step back and distill some of the key features and characteristics of OTC derivatives instruments, markets, and infrastructures. Ten such features can be identified that together convey the basic elements of modern banking and OTC derivatives activities and markets that are important for assessing market functioning, drawing implications for systemic financial risks, and identifying areas where improvements for ensuring financial stability might be obtained. The first two features address the risk characteristics of OTC derivatives and illustrate that OTC derivatives contracts are credit instruments that embody other risks, and that they can be used to unbundle, transform, and manage risk exposures. The next four features relate to the structure and operation of the markets, including the intermediation role of institutions active in these markets, the interbank/interdealer nature of the markets, the relatively high concentration of trading and counterparty risk exposures, and the central role OTC derivatives instruments and markets have come to play in other financial markets. The seventh and eighth features characterize OTC derivatives as vehicles that influence market liquidity and leverage. The last two features reflect characteristics of OTC markets that pose challenges for assessing and controlling both private and systemic risks, namely that OTC markets are relatively less transparent than other markets, and that they have become increasingly systemically important.

First, OTC derivative contracts are credit instruments. Even a simple plain vanilla interest-rate swap is a two-way credit instrument. For example, when two counterparts enter into an interest-rate swap, they trade cash flows associated with fixed and variable interest rate payments based on a notional value of the fixed-income instrument. While the principal (or notional value) of the contract is not at risk, the cash flows are, because they constitute a debt of one counterparty to the other. In addition, the stream of net cash payments varies with changes in the difference between the fixed and variable rates, giving rise to a potential future credit exposure (PFE).[95] As a result, the debtor/creditor relationship can vary over the life of the contract. One counterpart can be the net creditor (receiver of the cash flow) at the initiation of the contract, and because of changes in interest rates later become the net debtor (payer of the cash flow). In contrast, futures contracts do not embody much credit risk because the exchange or clearinghouse generally stands between counterparties and acts as a central counterparty for exchange-executed transactions by managing the credit risk through rules governing initial and variation margin, and settling defaults through loss-sharing arrangements.[96, 97] With OTC derivatives, the counterparties manage the bilateral creditor/debtor relationship, and incur the losses of default.

Second, OTC derivatives transform financial risks. They help financial institutions tailor, hedge, and manage risks with more precision and flexibility than can be achieved using other financial instruments, including exchange-traded derivatives. The capacity to unbundle, repackage, and transform risk provides increased opportunities for diversification and hedging of risk. It also makes it possible to separately price the different types of risk embodied in a financial instrument. This, in turn, enables institutions to select those types of risks they want to hold and hedge or sell those that they do not. In this way, OTC derivatives markets contribute to a more complete set of markets for trading and managing risk. Derivatives thus allow agents to tailor more precisely the risk characteristics of financial instruments to their risk preferences and tolerances. By contributing to more complete financial markets, derivatives can also improve market liquidity and increase the capacity of the financial system to bear risk and intermediate capital.

---

[95]See Box 3.5: Measuring Potential Future Exposure in a Swap Contract.

[96]Central clearinghouses for OTC derivatives, such as the London Clearing House's SwapClear and the OM Exchange's facility, have garnered little interest. See Box 4.2: Clearinghouses.

[97]Such a default could result in significant claims on other members of the clearinghouse, if the defaulting member's margin and the clearinghouse's own funds are exhausted.

To see this, consider the example of a company that issued a medium-term variable-rate bond last year expecting interest rates to decline, but that now expects interest rates to rise. The company can issue a new bond at a fixed interest rate and pay back the variable rate bond, but this may be too costly given prepayment penalties, underwriting fees, and other costs. Alternatively, the company can find a counterpart who expects interest rates to decline and is willing to pay (or receive) the difference between the variable and fixed rates. This is a swap, the most widely used OTC derivatives contract. In choosing the swap as its financing option, the company alters its risks and obligations in several key ways: while the company remains a (gross) debtor, it transforms the nature of its market risk; it now has to manage two cash flows (a variable-rate payment, and a fixed-rate receipt); and it becomes a (gross) creditor to the fixed-rate payer and has to manage the associated counterparty risk. The company may also decide to mitigate part of the counterparty risk by taking some collateral against the cash flow it is promised to receive, which adds operational complexity and some legal uncertainty. For example, if the paying counterpart goes bankrupt, the company might have to follow legally cumbersome closeout procedures for liquidating the position. This example of a plain vanilla swap illustrates how a simple OTC derivative can transform market risk into a combination of market, credit, and operational risks. In practice, financial intermediaries hold portfolios of OTC derivatives involving different combinations of these risks. To manage them effectively and take full advantage of their risk-transforming nature, sophisticated risk management and control systems are essential.

Third, the institutions that intermediate the bulk of transactions in OTC derivative markets are the large, internationally active financial institutions (see Table 2.1). These institutions also intermediate a large share of international capital flows and handle the lion's share of global lending, underwriting, mergers and acquisitions, and trading businesses. Their size, sophistication, diversification, and global reach give them a significant competitive advantage over smaller, more specialized institutions in the derivatives business. They have expanded and diversified their businesses in order to capture economies of scale and scope. These economies arise from the huge investments required to run a profitable global OTC derivatives business—in information and computer technologies, and in financial infrastructure—and from complementarities between OTC derivatives and other lines of business (for example, between fixed-income derivatives dealing and bond dealing and underwriting). As the head of a global OTC derivatives trading operation has stated, "the OTC derivatives business is like a team sport; you

can only be profitable if all aspects of the global business—sales, trading, back-office, information systems, risk management and control—are working effectively together." These global institutions are typically strongly capitalized, usually well-managed, and normally manage risk skillfully. They all have high credit ratings, which is critical for being viewed as a creditworthy counterparty in OTC derivatives transactions.

Fourth, OTC derivatives markets are essentially interbank and interdealer markets (similar to the major domestic money and foreign-exchange markets). The major institutions actively trade among themselves and make up a large share of the daily turnover in these markets. In 1998, for example, contracts between the major participants accounted for roughly one-half of notional principal in interest-rate derivatives (over half of the turnover) and one-third of notional principal in foreign-exchange derivatives (and about two-thirds of the turnover). This turnover results from two types of interbank and interdealer activity: the intermediation of derivatives transactions on behalf of clients—insurance companies, pension funds, asset management companies, hedge funds, and nonfinancial companies; and efforts by intermediaries to manage exposures and risks from these derivatives transactions with clients. For example, a large multinational corporation might ask a bank to arrange a swap out of a five-year variable-rate bond it issued in one currency a year ago into a fixed-rate bond in another currency for the remaining four years. The bank may enter the swap with the company even though it might not want the full exposure (that could entail many risks including interest-rate, foreign-exchange, and counterparty risk). It does so, in part, because it might expect a profit from one exposure (interest rate), and because it might need to build inventory in another type of instrument (for example, foreign exchange) in which it is a market maker. The bank therefore could unbundle the various components of exposures and risks, keep some of them for its own inventory and portfolio of risks, and sell off the remaining, often sizable, exposures to other counterparties that typically are the other internationally active financial institutions. In this way, a single transaction with an end-user can result in a large volume of interbank and interdealer hedging and rebalancing activity in many market segments.[98]

---

[98]Consider a $100 million interest-rate swap with an end-user client. If the intermediary wishes to hold only 10 percent of this exposure, it can enter an offsetting swap for $90 million with another intermediary. If, in turn, the second and each subsequent intermediary holds only 10 percent of each incoming transaction, in the limit, the initial $100 million swap gives rise to a $1 billion increase in notional outstandings and market turnover. Put differently, the initial $100 million "economically driven" transaction

Fifth, OTC derivatives markets are becoming concentrated among fewer but larger intermediaries. The level of concentration has increased over time, driven in large part by the economies of scale and scope required to be profitable in these highly efficient markets. This includes both a higher concentration of trading and counterparty exposures, in part because there are fewer counterparts with the capacity to hedge and rebalance OTC derivatives portfolios actively and profitably. Two recent examples of mergers that have increased this concentration are the merger between Deutsche Bank and Bankers Trust, both having very large and active global derivatives businesses, and the creation of Citigroup, which combines two active participants in OTC derivatives markets, Citicorp (a large commercial bank) and Salomon Smith Barney (a major securities house) with Travelers (a major insurance company). Moreover, smaller participants have been relatively inactive as intermediaries since the September 1998 market turbulence, and some former major participants (for example, Japanese banks) have scaled back their international OTC derivatives activities. Concentration may increase further if the pace of restructuring and consolidation picks up, particularly with the elimination of Glass-Steagall barriers between commercial and investment banks in the United States; the efforts to create "national champions" in Europe; and the creation of mega-banks in Japan.

Sixth, OTC derivatives markets are global and have become central to the efficient functioning of the international financial system. They closely link institutions, markets, and financial centers. They have become a major driving force behind the integration of national financial markets and the globalization of finance. The most obvious linkages arise from the contracts themselves. Currency swaps are used to transform currency risks and mobilize liquidity internationally across the major financial centers. Linkages also occur through the internationally active financial institutions that make up these markets. OTC derivatives markets also link the major dealing institutions, first through the array of market risks, and importantly, through a complex lattice of multiple, bilateral counterparty relationships between the major intermediaries. In addition, hedging, pricing, and arbitrage activities link OTC derivatives markets to the major cash and exchange-traded derivatives markets. For example, hedging and arbitrage activities link the market for interest-rate swaps and the

markets for bonds, interest-rate and bond futures, and interest-rate options. The interlinkages and the opportunities for arbitrage that they provide add to the efficiency and complexity of the international financial system.

Seventh, OTC derivatives can enhance or reduce market liquidity in different situations. Market liquidity allows participants to trade at prices that are not systematically affected by the size of the transaction, or technical market conditions. This makes it more likely that prices reflect fundamental demand and supply factors and increases economic and financial efficiency. OTC derivatives can support and enhance market liquidity. For example, because of their low cost and flexibility, OTC derivatives contracts are efficient vehicles for facilitating position taking and hedging. In effect, they are financing vehicles that augment other, more traditional mechanisms (like lines of credit) for maintaining and enhancing market liquidity. OTC derivatives activities can also be supportive of liquidity in related markets. Indeed, hedging of dollar interest-rate swaps has been credited with significantly improving market liquidity in the Eurodollar futures market. In other situations, OTC derivatives can absorb or reduce market liquidity. Because OTC derivatives involve extensions of credit, their financing—and refinancing when market conditions change—relies heavily on access to various sources of short-term credit, including interbank money markets and bank lines of credit. Situations can arise in which, for example, a rise in the cost of funding positions in a particular OTC derivatives market segment might make it too costly for a group of dealers trading in that market to continue to intermediate or carry particular OTC derivatives positions, and they might decide to reduce (temporarily) their level of activity. This would reduce turnover and liquidity in that segment, which in turn can reduce market liquidity overall. Given the relative size of OTC derivatives markets, a sharp reduction in activity can have a significant impact on market liquidity in related derivatives and spot markets.

Eighth, OTC derivatives contracts naturally embody leverage (see Box 5.1: Off-Balance-Sheet Leverage). For an individual investor, leverage enhances the potential return on an asset relative to capital. This can be achieved relatively easily and cheaply with OTC derivatives, in part because they are flexible credit instruments. For example, by buying an interest-rate swap—paying floating interest and receiving fixed interest—an investor can essentially buy a fixed-rate bond and finance it through a floating-rate loan, and thereby take a position on long-term interest rates for only a fraction of the amount that would be required to buy a long-term bond outright. The swap economizes on the use of

---

gave rise to $900 million in "financially driven" interdealer transactions, and correspondingly large gross (but smaller net) interdealer credit exposures. In foreign exchange markets, this has been called "hot-potato" trading. It partly explains why interbank foreign exchange turnover is much larger than the international trade and capital flows that it supports. See Lyons (1996).

Box 5.1. Off-Balance-Sheet Leverage

Leverage is the magnification of the rate of return (positive or negative) on a position or investment beyond the rate obtained by a direct investment of own funds in the cash market. Leverage is of concern because by definition it creates and enhances the risk of default by market participants; and it increases the potential for rapid deleveraging—the unwinding of leveraged positions—which can cause major disruptions in financial markets by exaggerating market movements.[1]

For private and systemic risk management, and market surveillance, it would be useful to have broad measures of the extent of leveraged positions in capital markets. This knowledge would allow market participants to assess the potential for rapid price movements resulting from exogenous adverse market shocks that may cause investors to deleverage in an attempt to mitigate their losses. Anticipation of possible turbulent deleveraging might limit the buildup of unsustainable leverage. Hence, a publicly available measure for overall leverage by institutions and in markets could enhance self-stabilizing forces without necessitating disclosure of proprietary position data to the public. Since leverage in modern financial markets can easily be assumed by using derivative contracts, it is useful to have a measure that not only captures on-balance-sheet leverage but also the leverage implicit in off-balance-sheet transactions. Despite the importance of leverage, empirical measures of leverage are difficult to implement.

Leverage is traditionally measured by the ratio of a firm's total assets relative to its equity. Calculating this ratio is straightforward if the firm only relies on balance-sheet transactions, such as bank loans. However, if the firm uses off-balance-sheet transactions, such as derivative instruments, the measurement of leverage is more complicated. This box first explains how the leverage that is implied by the most common derivative instruments could be measured. More complicated derivatives, such as swaps and structured notes, can generally be decomposed into spot market, forward, and option positions and will therefore not be considered separately. The box also presents methods for aggregating leverage within an institution and within markets.[2]

Leverage Implicit in Plain Vanilla Derivative Instruments

To assess leverage resulting from a derivative contract, the contract can be decomposed into its cash market equivalent components. The basic derivative instruments—forwards and options—can be replicated by holding (and, in the case of options, constantly adjusting) positions in the spot market of the underlying security, and by borrowing or lending in the money market. This replication of the contract maps the individual components into own-funds equivalents (equity) and borrowed-funds equivalents (debt), which can be used to measure the leverage contained in long and short forward positions and option contracts.

Consider, as an example, a long forward contract on a security that, for simplicity, provides no (interest or dividend) income. Purchasing a security forward is equivalent to borrowing cash at the risk-free interest rate, supplementing the borrowed funds with own funds in the amount that would otherwise be spent on the forward contract, and investing the total amount in the underlying asset. In the replicating portfolio, own funds are equivalent to the market value of the contract;[3] the sum of own and borrowed funds is equivalent to the contract's current notional value.[4] Hence, the leverage ratio implicit in a forward contract is defined as the current notional value relative to the contract's market value. As a short forward position is tantamount to a short position in the underlying asset, its leverage ratio—defined in the same way as that of a long forward ratio—is negative. To compare leverage ratios for short positions and long positions, it is therefore necessary to take the absolute value of leverage ratios for short positions. Leverage ratios for long and short option positions can be calculated in a similar fashion (see table).

As the price of the underlying asset changes, the value of the forward contract—and thus the value of equity—will change, which implies a continually changing leverage ratio. This is similar to on-balance-sheet leverage: as the value of the underlying security increases (decreases), the investor's equity rises at a faster rate than the value of the assets, thereby reducing the leverage ratio; and vice versa. The leverage ratio could ultimately reach infinity when losses equal the equity in the position.[5] However, for exchange-traded derivatives the ratio is bounded as a result of margin requirements. Futures margin requirements range between 2 percent, implying a maximum leverage ratio of 50, and 8 percent, implying a maximum ratio of 12.5. Although leverage in forward contracts

---

[1]See International Monetary Fund (1998b), Box 3.3, and Breuer (2000).

[2]Leverage has the capacity to increase risk. For a given equity base, leverage allows the borrower to build up a larger investment position and thus higher exposure to market risk. Since leverage increases the potential loss triggered by a given adverse price movement, leveraged investors are likely to adjust their positions sooner than pure equity investors. The simultaneous unwinding of large leveraged positions may, in turn, trigger further price movements and therefore increase risk.

[3]The market value of a derivatives contract, in turn, might be financed by on-balance-sheet debt and on-balance-sheet equity.

[4]The current notional value of a derivative contract is defined as the product of the number of underlying shares and their current market price. By contrast, the notional amount refers to the product of the number of underlying shares and the delivery (exercise) price specified in the contract.

[5]Note that the leverage ratio in this box is defined to remain at infinity when losses exceed equity, even though the mathematical ratio would change signs.

Leverage Ratios in Basic Derivative Instruments

Derivative	Long Position	Short Position
Forward contract	current notional value	– current notional value
	market value of contract	market value of contract
Call option[1]	(delta) x (current notional value)	– (delta) x (current notional value)
	option price	option price
Put option[2]	– (delta) x (current notional value)	(delta) x (current notional value)
	option price	option price

[1]The "delta" of an option—also called the "hedge ratio"—is defined as the rate of change of the option price with respect to the price of the underlying asset.

[2] The delta of a put option, Δ_t^p, is related to the delta of an equivalent call option ($\Delta_t^p = \Delta_t^c - 1$).

is typically not bounded by margin requirements, it may be limited by overall credit and trading limits that institutions have with each other.

Aggregate Leverage of a Financial Institution

The mapped asset components can be aggregated for an institution and expressed relative to its on-balance-sheet equity. There are at least two ways of aggregating assets to arrive at an overall measure of leverage for a financial institution: the "gross leverage ratio" and the "net leverage ratio." Both ratios add the spot market asset equivalent components in some form to on-balance-sheet assets before dividing by on-balance-sheet equity.[6] To the extent that the institution's overall equity is positive, the leverage ratio will be less than infinity, even though some of its positions may have infinite leverage.

The "gross leverage ratio" adds the absolute amount of short (negative) asset equivalents to that of long (positive) positions. Hence, this ratio, in general, overstates the total market exposure as short positions may offset long positions to some extent. Subtracting short asset positions from long asset positions yields the "net leverage ratio," which is smaller than the gross leverage ratio. Both ratios measure the relationship between

an investor's exposure and that investor's equity. While the net leverage ratio may more accurately reflect the market risk of a leveraged investor, it does not take into account credit and liquidity risk inherent in the individual contracts. By contrast, the gross leverage ratio incorporates all those risks.

As a third measure of leverage, the U.S. President's Working Group on Financial Markets proposed the value at risk of an entity's portfolio relative to its equity. This is not, however, a measure of leverage per se. Rather, it is a measure of risk and addresses whether an institution's equity is sufficient to cover potential losses due to market risk. Hence, it could be called the "risk coverage ratio." Unlike the leverage ratio, this ratio does not capture the extent to which the institution has pooled economic resources from outside debt investors and therefore its systemic importance. To judge the "riskiness" of an institution it would be useful to know all three ratios.[7] Regulators are currently considering whether disclosure of these ratios ought to be required.

It is impossible to precisely measure leverage for institutions active in derivative markets without full knowledge of their positions, including hedges. However, data filed by commercial banks and trust companies in the United States with the Office of the Comptroller of the Currency allow an approximation. As gross market values of derivative positions (not subject to netting) are itemized as assets and liabilities on the balance sheet, changes in the value of these positions directly affect the firm's equity. Hence, the ratio of current notional values outstanding to the equity of the institution indicates the extent of off-balance-sheet gross leverage. The sum of this ratio and the conventional balance sheet leverage ratio can serve as an approximation to the overall gross leverage ratio. The net leverage ratio cannot be calculated without further information about the nature of the positions.

Gross off-balance-sheet leverage of the top 25 U.S. banks, which in June 2000 held approximately 99 percent of the total notional amount of derivatives in the domestic banking system and 41 percent of derivatives outstanding worldwide, exceeded the leverage of the remaining domestic commercial banks by a wide margin.[8] For the latter group the ratio ranged around 0.1, indicating virtually no derivatives activity.[9] In the after-

---

[6]Alternatively, the off-balance-sheet gross and net leverage ratios could be calculated by dividing the sum of asset equivalent components by the sum of equity equivalent components. Positions that have an infinite leverage ratio will contribute only to the numerator and not to the denominator.

[7]Two important shortcomings are that these ratios, by their nature, need to be reported by the financial institutions themselves and that the VaR data are predicated on very specific assumptions.

[8]Risk-based capital, the sum of Tier 1 and Tier 2 capital, was derived from data from the Office of the Comptroller of the Currency.

[9]The reported figures overstate the gross leverage ratio because the "delta" of option contracts is assumed to be 1 (owing to lack of data) and because the reported notional amounts are valued at exercise (delivery) prices, and not at current market prices.

Box 5.1 (concluded)

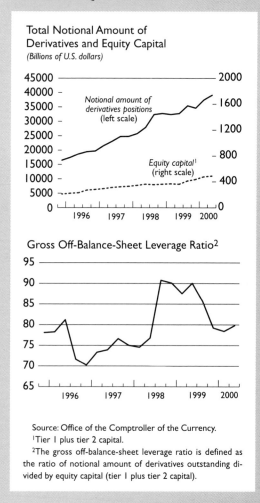

United States: Top 25 Commercial Banks—Notional Amount of Derivatives, Equity Capital, and the Gross Off-Balance-Sheet Leverage Ratio, Fourth Quarter 1995–Second Quarter 2000

Total Notional Amount of Derivatives and Equity Capital
(Billions of U.S. dollars)

Gross Off-Balance-Sheet Leverage Ratio[2]

Source: Office of the Comptroller of the Currency.
[1]Tier 1 plus tier 2 capital.
[2]The gross off-balance-sheet leverage ratio is defined as the ratio of notional amount of derivatives outstanding divided by equity capital (tier 1 plus tier 2 capital).

third quarter of 1998.[10] The increase was largely due to an upsurge in derivatives exposures rather than a decrease in capital (see the figure). In contrast, traditional balance sheet leverage ranged between 6 and 7 during the same period. While the gross leverage ratio only provides an upper bound to net leverage, the relative movements confirm the concentration of off-balance-sheet leverage among a few banks and a significant increase of leverage during the third quarter of 1998. In the second half of 1999, the gross leverage ratio declined to around the levels that prevailed at mid–1998.

Leverage in Markets

To determine the potential for financial market turbulence stemming from deleveraging it is useful to estimate the extent of leveraged positions in a particular market. In practice, it is not possible to gather such data without individual position data, particularly for off-balance-sheet transactions. However, the BIS survey of derivatives market activity allows approximations of the extent of leverage in certain derivatives markets on a global basis. The survey reports total gross notional amounts and total gross market values outstanding in various segments of the foreign exchange derivative and interest rate derivative markets at semiannual intervals. Notional amounts are aggregated in a similar fashion as suggested for the gross leverage ratio. Based on the definitions of leverage introduced above, the notional amounts outstanding divided by the gross market value approximates the gross leverage ratio.[11]

The data indicate that the overall approximate gross leverage ratio increased from 22 in 1995 to 36 in 2000 (see table). Interest rate derivative contracts had higher leverage ratios than foreign exchange derivative contracts, reflecting the fact that the latter—unlike the former—typically involve an exchange of principal. In addition, interest rates tend to be less volatile than exchange rates, so that market values of interest rate contracts (for a given notional amount) tend to be smaller than those of foreign exchange contracts. The latter also represent exposure to both currency and interest rate risks, which also contributes to a higher market value relative to the notional amount. The reported high degree of leverage in option contracts overstates actual leverage because of the implicit assumption of delta being unity.

---

[10]One globally active bank reached a ratio as high as 579.
[11]See footnote 9.

math of the 1996 bond market turbulence and the associated deleveraging, leverage among the top 25 banks increased gradually from 70 in 1996 until the second quarter of 1998. It surged by 18 percent to 91 in the

up-front capital in taking the risk—freeing capital for other transactions—and enhances the return (or loss) relative to the capital invested. If interest rates fall, the swap (like a long-term bond) appreciates in value, and the investor receives a relatively high return on invested capital; if interest rates rise, the swap depreciates in value, and the investor will probably be required to put up more capital or borrow again to make the additional payment, and thereby will experience a loss relative to invested

Global Positions and Approximate Gross Leverage Ratios in Over-the-Counter Derivatives Markets by Type of Risk Instruments[1]
(Billions of U.S. dollars)

	Notional Amounts		Gross Market Value		Approximate Gross Leverage Ratio		
	End-Mar. 1995	End-June 2000	End-Mar. 1995	End-June 2000	End-Mar. 1995	End-June 2000	Percent change
Foreign exchange contracts	13,095	15,494	1,048	578	12	27	115
Outright forward and forex swaps	8,699	10,504	622	283	14	37	165
Currency swaps	1,957	2,605	346	239	6	11	93
Options	2,379	2,385	71	55	34	43	29
Other	61	...	10	...	6	...	...
Memorandum item:							
Exchange-traded contracts	119	51	...	...	...	...	...
Interest rate contracts[2]	26,645	64,125	647	1,230	41	52	27
FRAs	4,597	6,771	18	13	255	521	104
Swaps	18,283	47,993	562	1,072	33	45	38
Options	3,548	9,361	60	145	59	65	9
Other	216	...	7	...	31	...	...
Memorandum item:							
Exchange-traded contracts	9,722	12,313	...	...	...	...	...
Equity-linked contracts	579	1,671	50	293	12	6	−51
Forwards and swaps	52	348	7	62	7	6	−24
Options	527	1,323	43	231	12	6	−53
Commodities contracts[3]	318	584	28	80	11	7	−36
Gold	147	262	10	19	15	14	−6
Other	171	323	18	61	10	5	−44
Forwards and swaps	120	169	13	...	9	...	...
Options	51	154	5	...	10	...	...
Other	...	12,163	...	400	...	30	...
Estimated gaps in reporting	6,893	...	432	...	...	...	...
Total contracts	47,530	94,037	2,205	2,581	22	36	69

Source: Bank for International Settlements.

[1]All figures are adjusted for double-counting. Notional amounts outstanding have been adjusted by halving positions vis-à-vis other reporting dealers. Gross market values have been calculated as the sum of the total gross positive market value of contracts and the absolute value of gross negative market value of contracts with non-reporting counterparties.

[2]Single-currency contracts only.

[3]Adjustments for double-counting are estimated.

capital. Thus, compared with an outright (unleveraged) investment in the underlying asset, the leveraged investment in an OTC derivatives contract has greater upside potential, but it also embodies higher risk relative to the capital invested, and it can put at risk the investor's overall capital if it is not well managed. Taking this example to the level of the market, the more active and liquid is the swap market, the greater is the likelihood that long-term bonds will also trade in a liquid market. This is because swaps allow risks associated with long-term bonds to be precisely hedged or leveraged, and this makes bonds attractive to a larger set of investors. However, the implied leverage in the swap market can magnify the effect of changes in the bond market.

Ninth, OTC derivatives activities are relatively opaque. In traditional banking, when a bank issues a loan the risks are transparent even if they are not easily quantified and managed. With OTC derivatives transactions, it can be difficult to adequately gauge, assess and understand the distribution and balance of counterparty and other risks, including who owns which risks. Part of this lack of transparency originates in the ability of derivatives to unbundle and repackage separate components of risk. Opacity also reflects the organization of the market. In general, interbank and interdealer markets lack transparency except for actively engaged market participants. Major OTC derivatives intermediaries receive information about the distribution of risks and exposures by observing order flows, but they closely guard this information. In addition, transparency is much more limited in OTC deals than in exchange-traded transactions, in part because OTC derivatives deals are bilateral individual transactions.

Tenth, OTC derivatives markets are systemically important. Their systemic importance arises from two key characteristics of OTC markets and the intermediaries active in them. First, given the concentrated nature of OTC markets, the major players are a large enough share of the market to cause a market disruption if they were to encounter liquidity or solvency problems (especially those not part of the safety net). Second, in the event a global (and necessarily large) financial institution encountered a solvency problem, while the institution might not be too big or complex to close or liquidate, it might be too big to close and liquidate quickly without potentially causing a market disruption. This reflects the fact that global institutions have large balance sheets and similarly large off-balance-sheet positions. They are active in, and in the aggregate, largely comprise a wide variety of cash securities markets, interbank lending markets, and other international financial markets, and may span several legal and regulatory jurisdictions. They play a critical role in intermediat-

ing savings and international capital flows, and in supporting economic activity in an increasingly interconnected global economic and financial system. As these institutions are well aware of the public's interest in these considerations, authorities consider it critical to strike a balance between establishing mechanisms to ensure soundness and limiting the moral hazard that such measures might engender. In this connection, and owing to the complex nature of these markets and institutions, authorities rely on market discipline.

These ten features highlight characteristics of OTC derivatives markets that distinguish them from other markets in four key areas: risks, structure, their financing role, and financial stability. Concerning risks, OTC derivatives have a unique capacity to transform and tailor risk but this gives rise to credit and other exposures that must be managed. More generally, the greater complexity of risks that results from their use requires sophisticated and effective risk management systems if the benefits of OTC derivatives markets are to be fully realized. What distinguishes the structure of OTC derivatives markets is that they depend on a relatively small number of large, globally active institutions to intermediate transactions and provide liquidity. Moreover, they are becoming more concentrated over time due to rising economies of scale and scope driven largely by technology. They play a central role linking financial institutions, markets, and centers thereby contributing to the globalization of the financial system. Regarding the financing role, OTC derivatives are efficient financial vehicles that contribute to market liquidity and can be used for leverage. Because they involve extensions of credit, the extent of their financing role depends on credit conditions and liquidity in money markets and bank financing. Important from a financial stability perspective, OTC derivatives markets are distinguished by their lack of transparency about who owns what risks. Finally, the large size of the active institutions and the concentration and complexity of the exposures to one another makes OTC derivatives markets systemically important. All of these key features bear importantly on the related financial stability issues discussed in the next section.

VI Financial Stability Issues in Modern Banking: Sources of Financial Instability and Structural Weakness in OTC Derivatives Activities

As noted in the previous sections, some of the features of OTC derivatives contracts and markets that provide benefits and enhance efficiency either separately or jointly embody risks to financial market stability. OTC derivatives activities are governed almost exclusively by decentralized private infrastructures (including risk management and control systems, private netting arrangements, and closeout procedures) and market-disciplining mechanisms. By comparison, the more formal centralized rules of exchanges protect the stability and financial integrity of the exchange. In addition, the major financial intermediaries in OTC derivatives markets have access to financial safety nets. Because this can affect their behavior, they are required to adhere to prudential regulations and standards in the form of minimum risk-adjusted capital requirements and accounting and disclosure standards that inform financial stakeholders and to some extent support market discipline. The financial industry also has its own standards and best practices promulgated by various industry groups.

Private, decentralized mechanisms have so far safeguarded the soundness of the internationally active financial institutions, in part because many of them have been well capitalized. However, these mechanisms did not adequately protect market stability, and markets and countries only remotely related to derivatives activities experienced instability because of spillovers and contagion. For example, while no major institution failed during the mature markets turbulence of 1998 surrounding the near-collapse of LTCM, private, decentralized market-disciplining mechanisms failed to prevent the buildup and concentration of counterparty risk exposures within the internationally active financial institutions.

Sources of Instability in OTC Derivatives Activities and Markets

The features of OTC derivatives markets that can give rise to instability in institutions, markets, and the international financial system include the dynamic nature of gross credit exposures; information asymmetries; the effects of OTC derivatives activities on available aggregate credit; the high concentration of OTC derivatives activities in the major institutions; and the central role of OTC derivatives markets in the global financial system.

The first underlying source of market instability is the dynamic nature of gross credit exposures, which are sensitive to changes in information about counterparties and asset prices. This feature played an important role in most of the crises in the 1990s. A disruption that sharply raises credit exposures has the capacity to cause sudden and extreme liquidity demands (to meet margin calls, for example). Just as traditional banks were not always prepared for sudden abnormally large liquidity demands and withdrawals of deposits during bank runs, today's derivatives market participants may not be prepared for sudden and abnormally large demands for cash that can and do arise in periods of market stress.

A second, well-known and related, source is information asymmetries, as in traditional banking.[99] Not having sufficient information on borrowers complicates the assessment of counterparty risks. This problem is exaggerated for the credit exposures associated with OTC instruments because of the price-dependent, time-varying nature of these credit exposures. A counterparty's risk profile can change very quickly in OTC derivatives markets. As a result, information asymmetries in OTC derivatives markets can be more destabilizing than in traditional banking markets because they can quickly lead intermediaries and market makers to radically scale back exposures, risk taking, and the amount of capital committed to intermediary and market-making functions.

Third, OTC derivatives activities contribute to the aggregate amount of credit available for financing, and also to market liquidity in underlying asset markets. The capacity for the internationally active institutions to expand and contract off-balance-

---

[99]See Diamond (1984).

sheet credit depends on the amount of *capital* they jointly devote to intermediation and market making in derivatives markets. This capital can support more or less activity depending on several factors, including the risk tolerances (amount of leveraging) of the intermediaries and market makers; the underlying cost of internal capital or external financing; and financial-sector policies (for example, capital requirements). A determinant of the cost of capital for OTC derivatives activities is the risk-free interest rate (such as on 10-year U.S. Treasury bonds), which is also used for pricing contracts. When underlying financing conditions become favorable, the OTC-intermediation activities can become more profitable and more cheaply funded and the level of activity can expand relative to the base of equity capital in the financial system. This tendency for expansion (and, when conditions change, contraction) can become self-generating, and it can, and has, occasionally become hypersensitive to changes in market conditions.

Fourth, as noted, aggregate OTC derivatives activities are sizable and the trading activity ($1 trillion daily turnover) and counterparty exposures are highly concentrated in the internationally active financial institutions. This makes the institutions and global markets susceptible to a range of shocks and dynamics that impinge on one or more major counterparties. The reason for this concentration is clear. Profitability requires large-scale investments in information technologies (such as sophisticated risk management systems) and also requires a broad client base and the ability to deal in a wide variety of related cash products. Only the largest organizations with global reach and international networks of clients and distribution channels can effectively compete as the central players in OTC markets. As a result, intermediation and market making are performed by global institutions, who hold and manage the attendant risks through, among other methods, hedging and trading. The major intermediaries have access to financial safety nets, which may impart an element of subsidy in the pricing of credit and other risks. This is problematic because it could contribute to an overextension of credit. This concentration makes OTC derivatives markets and the institutions trading in them potentially vulnerable to sudden changes in market prices for underlying assets (for example, interest rates and exchange rates) and in the general market appetite for risk.

Fifth, OTC derivatives activities closely link institutions, markets, and financial centers. This makes them possible vehicles for spillovers and contagion. About half or more of OTC derivatives trading in the largest segments takes place across national borders. Linkages arise from the contracts themselves (currency swaps mobilize liquidity across the major international financial centers) and also through the international institutions that make up these markets. In addition, hedging, pricing, and arbitrage activities link OTC derivatives markets to the major cash and exchange-traded derivatives markets: for example, hedging and arbitrage activities link the market for interest rate swaps and the markets for bonds, interest rate and bond futures, and interest rate options. The interlinkages and the opportunities for arbitrage that they provide add to the efficiency and complexity of the international financial system. At the same time, interlinkages also mean that disruptions in OTC activities necessarily entail spillovers and contagion to these other markets.

To summarize, certain features of OTC derivatives and how they are traded and managed make OTC derivatives markets subject to instability if the wrong combination of circumstances arises. This instability arises, in part, because OTC derivatives markets are centered around the internationally active financial institutions that each are counterparty to tens of thousands of bilateral, price-dependent, dynamic credit exposures embodied in OTC derivatives contracts. OTC derivatives contracts bind institutions together in an opaque network of credit exposures, the size and characteristics of which can change rapidly and, moreover, are arguably not fully understood with a high degree of accuracy even by market participants themselves. These institutions allocate specific amounts of capital to support their perceived current and potential future credit exposures in their OTC derivatives business. However, risk assessments and management of these exposures are seriously complicated by a lack of solid information and risk analyses about the riskiness of both their own positions and those of their counterparties. As a result, this market is characterized by informational imperfections about current and potential future credit exposures and market-wide financial conditions.

The potential for instability arises when information shocks, especially counterparty credit events and sharp movements in asset prices that underlie derivative contracts, cause significant changes in perceptions of current and potential future credit exposures. Changes in perceptions, in turn, can cause very large movements in derivatives positions of the major participants. When asset prices adjust rapidly, the size and configuration of counterparty exposures can become unsustainably large and provoke a rapid unwinding of positions. Recent experience strongly suggests that the ebb and flow of credit exposures among the large internationally active financial institutions can be severely affected by some events, which cannot be easily predicted and which can lead to potentially disruptive systemic consequences.

Weaknesses in the Infrastructure

There are also aspects of the infrastructure for OTC derivatives activities that can lead to a breakdown in the effectiveness of market discipline and ultimately produce unsustainable market conditions and affect market dynamics, including producing or exacerbating underlying instabilities through inadequate counterparty risk management; limited understandings of market dynamics and liquidity risk; and legal and regulatory uncertainty. All of these areas can be improved through efforts, separately or jointly, by financial institutions, supervisors, and market surveillance.

Inadequate Counterparty Risk Management

Although counterparty risk is now widely understood to be of primary importance, discussions with internationally active financial institutions and supervisory authorities suggest that limited progress has been made so far in improving the management of credit risk associated with OTC derivatives.[100] Progress has been particularly slow in developing techniques for managing the interactions of credit and market risk. Even less well understood are the interactions with liquidity, operational, and legal risk.

Several factors explain this limited progress. First, counterparty disclosure has not improved significantly since 1998. The leading providers of intermediation and market-making services in OTC derivatives markets have serious concerns about the dearth of information supplied by clients. Second, the conceptual and measurement challenges involved in understanding counterparty risk and other risks are unlikely to be resolved soon. Even sophisticated institutions acknowledge that significant additional progress is necessary.

Widespread problems with ex-ante counterparty risk assessment and pricing produced turbulence in OTC derivatives markets, in part because incentives for prudent risk taking proved to be insufficient to prevent the buildup and concentration of counterparty risk exposures in the autumn of 1998. After the turbulence, however, some of these same incentives worked better, including the discipline from losses in shareholder value and the associated lower bonuses for managers, and the discipline imposed by senior management in determining the risk culture, in setting risk tolerances, and in implementing risk management and control systems. Thus, experience in the LTCM affair appears to have taught some valuable lessons. It remains to be seen, however, if

corrections that are being implemented will prove adequate in the future.

If information to assess creditworthiness is insufficient, the reliance on collateral is generally a reasonable counterparty-risk-mitigation technique. However, the assets held as collateral are subject to market risk and their value can decline precipitously when the protection they offer is most needed, namely, during periods of turbulence when the probability of counterparty default can rise significantly. This risk may not have been adequately accounted for in the management of OTC derivatives trading books.

Institutions acknowledge that there were inadequacies in collateral management and uncertainties about legal claims on collateral. Both contributed to market turbulence in the 1990s by encouraging financial institutions to liquidate collateral into declining markets. In addition, in the run-up to the turbulence of the autumn of 1998, counterparties tended to demand low or no haircuts on collateral, because of competitive pressures and the relatively low cost of funding at that time. These measures could have offered protection against declines in collateral values and helped to reduce pressures to liquidate collateral into declining markets.

According to internationally active financial institutions, globally integrated collateral management systems are being developed to overcome some of these difficulties. But only large institutions can afford, develop, and utilize them. Discussions with market participants suggest that it will most likely take some time (another 12 months from June 2000) before any of the leaders in this field have such systems up and running. Second-tier institutions, including most hedge funds, seem to have fallen further behind in the application of risk-management tools, which may partly explain why some hedge funds have recently withdrawn from some markets and scaled back highly leveraged activities.

Limited Understanding of Market Dynamics and Liquidity Risks

Market participants and officials acknowledge they have a limited understanding of market dynamics in OTC derivatives markets and their implications for related markets. Views diverge on whether OTC markets absorb financial shocks or whether they amplify shocks and contribute to volatility. Some believe derivatives markets dissipate shocks by facilitating hedging, while others see these markets as a channel of contagion. Market participants also disagree about how OTC derivatives markets affect the distribution and mix of credit, market, liquidity, operational, and legal risks. One view is that they redistribute risks to those most willing to hold

---

[100]See Counterparty Risk Management Policy Group (1999).

them. Another is that they transform risks in ways that are inherently more difficult to manage because, while reducing market risk, they create credit, operational, and legal risk. Views on relationships between liquidity in derivatives, secondary, and money markets vary considerably. Finally, there is widespread uncertainty about how monetary conditions influence prices and liquidity in OTC derivatives markets.

Market participants acknowledge that they failed to realize the importance of liquidity risk in OTC derivatives, and that the capacity to manage it is still in an embryonic stage. One common mistake was that risk management systems assumed that markets would remain liquid and price changes would follow historical norms. Risk managers also failed to engage in stress testing that examined the implications of severe liquidity problems. Few firms were, for the purposes of risk management, marking credit exposures to estimated liquidation values instead of to current market values. Even these firms seemed to rely on stress tests that did not fully capture the dynamics that were revealed in 1998.

Marking positions to liquidation values is likely to become standard practice at sophisticated financial institutions. However, liquidation values may not be uniquely determined, because asset prices are widely seen as behaving in nonlinear ways at stress points. Thus, even sophisticated institutions will make modeling errors. Less sophisticated firms may rely on margining requirements and haircuts. But this too has its limitations in times of stress: reliance on margin calls to limit counterparty credit risk, normally an effective risk management tool, also can contribute to liquidity pressures in apparently unrelated markets and can raise the likelihood of default by financial institutions that would be solvent under normal market conditions. Likewise, over-reliance on VaR and mark-to-market accounting, and other rules that encourage frequent portfolio rebalancing, can induce large-scale selling of positions.[101]

To address the challenges posed by liquidity risks and market dynamics, sophisticated institutions are beginning to focus on the total risk they face rather than on the individual risks (market, credit, liquidity, operational, and legal risk) separately. Particularly challenging is the link between liquidity and counterparty risk, which may depend on the underlying trading, risk-mitigation, and legal infrastructure. Liquidity risk can become closely linked to credit risk, because a loss of liquidity can depress market prices and increase the credit exposure on OTC derivatives. Conversely, heightened concerns about counterparty credit risk can precipitate a loss of liquidity by causing market participants to pull back from markets. International financial institutions recognize the need to incorporate linkages into risk management systems, and the formidable challenges of measuring and modeling them. The September 1998 market turbulence may have been the first event that revealed the importance of these linkages, so institutions may still lack sufficient experience to incorporate them into their stress tests in a reliable way. Future improvements in the management of total risk should contribute to the smooth functioning of OTC derivatives markets.

Legal and Regulatory Uncertainties

Another important source of weakness in the financial infrastructure is legal and regulatory uncertainty. This type of uncertainty encompasses the possibility that private arrangements to mitigate risks (such as definitions of default and legality of closeout and netting arrangements) may turn out to be ineffective. To the extent that risk mitigation fails to work as designed, misperceptions, mispricing, and misallocation of financial risk can result. Legal and regulatory uncertainties can also be important sources of liquidity risk, because they can contribute to adverse market dynamics.

Cumbersome closeout procedures and uncertain enforcement of security interests in collateral can be impractical and ineffective in protecting firms against default. According to market participants, such concerns contributed to the rapid liquidation of collateral in the autumn of 1998. But closeout procedures are as legally uncertain now as they were then. The uncertainty arises because of important differences in bankruptcy laws among countries. Specifically, a number of countries do not allow the termination of contracts upon the initiation of insolvency proceedings, giving the trustee the opportunity to continue those contracts that are favorable to the estate ("cherry picking"). Moreover, even among countries that allow for the termination of contracts, some do not allow for the automatic set-off of contractual claims, which is necessary for netting and closeout. Regarding the enforceability of security interests in collateral, there is a growing convergence among national bankruptcy laws to allow for the stay on the enforcement of security interests. In these cases, the law will often provide that the interest of secured creditors will be protected during the stay (for example, by compensating for the depreciation of the value of the collateral). One uncertainty that arises in many countries is whether such protection will be provided and, if so, whether it will be adequate.

When market participants cannot close out positions or reclaim collateral as specified in private

---

[101]See Schinasi and Smith (1999).

contracts, collateral does not give the expected protection against credit risk. When this is realized in "real time," credit risk can quickly cross a threshold and is perceived as a default event. With this kind of uncertainty, firms holding collateral with creditor-stay exemptions (which allow counterparties to close out exempt OTC derivative transactions outside of bankruptcy procedures) have the incentive to exercise their legal right to sell collateral. Closeout valuations require three to five market quotes per contract, and a derivatives desk may have thousands of contracts with a single counterparty. A dealer attempting to close out roughly the number of swaps with LTCM might have had to collect 16,000 market quotes from other dealers at a time of market stress when every other major desk was attempting to do the same. It would be an improvement to permit alternative valuation procedures, including good-faith estimates, internal valuations, or replacement value, and this possibility was still under discussion two years after the near-collapse of LTCM.

Widely used netting agreements (such as the ISDA master agreement) have limitations in mitigating risk. Netting arrangements can reduce the credit exposures on a large number of transactions between two counterparties to a single net figure. As such they are a risk-mitigating technique with significant potential to reduce large gross credit exposures. If netting cannot be relied upon as legally enforceable, the hint of default can trigger the unwinding of gross exposures. The failure to recognize this possibility may be a source of misperceptions of risk. Several initiatives are currently under way to facilitate bilateral and multilateral netting, but they are typically only for specific instruments (for example, RepoClear).

Significant uncertainties also exist about the various legal and regulatory environments in which OTC derivatives transactions are conducted, owing to the high pace of innovation, the relatively limited extent of legal precedent, the cross-border nature of OTC derivatives markets, and the supervisory and regulatory framework. Legal risks include the possibility that a counterparty may "walk away" from obligations, or may cherry pick; it may dispute the terms of an agreement; it may claim that it did not understand the agreement; and it may claim that it did not have the authority to enter into the agreement.

In the United States, there is legal ambiguity about whether certain types of swaps are subject to CFTC approval and oversight. This has contributed to reluctance to standardize swap contracts and to centralize clearing.[102] Some market participants believe there is also a need to modernize bankruptcy procedures to strengthen the legal certainty of risk-mitigation methods and the definitions of what constitutes a default, which is particularly relevant for the development of credit derivatives. For example, some see a need to extend creditor-stay exemptions under U.S. bankruptcy law beyond swaps and repurchase transactions to other OTC derivatives contracts.

Outside U.S. and U.K. laws, many jurisdictions are ill-suited for effective modern risk management. For example, collateral may afford limited protection in bankruptcy (unless the collateral is held in these two jurisdictions). Legal staffs at major dealer and market-making institutions see significant legal uncertainties associated with the use of collateral in advanced countries (Canada, Italy, and Japan). While the legal and regulatory environments for OTC derivatives are complex in the United States and the United Kingdom they are considerably more complicated elsewhere. The same instrument might be legally defined as a swap transaction in one country, an insurance contract in a second country, and a pari-mutuel-betting instrument in a third country. Market participants are making strong efforts to mitigate the legal risks, but there are limits to what the private sector can accomplish because contracts must ultimately be enforceable in a legal system.

---

[102]See Folkerts-Landau and Steinherr (1994).

VII   Strengthening the Stability of Modern Banking and OTC Derivatives Markets

Market participants and officials acknowledge there are problems, if not instabilities, and weaknesses in OTC derivatives markets, and proposals and initiatives have been advanced. Some progress has already been made, and the lessons of recent experience are likely to motivate further actions. However, the available evidence suggests that many recognized problems have yet to be adequately addressed. Insufficient progress has been made in implementing reforms in risk management, including counterparty, liquidity, and operational risks.[103] Relatively less attention has been focused on removing legal and regulatory uncertainty. Given the limited progress to date, it is essential to implement changes to reduce market instability.

Balancing Private and Official Roles

Many of the instabilities identified above can be seen as imperfections in three areas: market discipline, risk-mitigating infrastructures, and official rule making and oversight. Aspects of all three failed to prevent the buildup and concentration of counterparty exposures in 1998. Strengthening market stability requires improvements in each of these three areas, but consideration should also be given to altering the balance of the roles of the private and public sectors in ensuring market stability, in particular in tilting the balance in the direction of greater reliance on effective market discipline. It is in the general public's interest to have these markets function as smoothly as possible most, if not all, of the time. This raises the more general question: what is the appropriate balance of market discipline on the one hand, and official oversight on the other hand, for ensuring the smooth functioning of OTC derivatives markets?

In striking this balance several factors are relevant. The authorities in the mature markets, primar-

ily through G–10 efforts, have collectively more or less adopted an approach that places as heavy a reliance on market discipline as is feasible, while recognizing the limits to private discipline, including those emanating from moral hazard, information asymmetries, and other externalities. There is less agreement on the desirable degree of official involvement. Nevertheless, a strong case can be made for relying more heavily on market disciplining mechanisms provided they can be made more effective. There may also be areas of complementarities and scope for constructive engagement. One such area is disclosure; more voluntary and some involuntary disclosure might go a long way toward improving the effectiveness of risk management and market discipline through greater financial stakeholder awareness. But only the right kind of disclosure would improve matters, and the international community is not clear about the kind or frequency of information that is required. Another consideration is that there are tradeoffs. For example, more official oversight or regulation, by creating the impression that officials are monitoring, can create moral hazard by diminishing private stakeholder incentives to monitor and influence business decisions and reduce management incentives for prudent risk taking. Striking the right balance needs to take account of these interrelated effects.

If it is desirable that market discipline carry the heaviest load, it would seem necessary to identify more rigorously the limits (natural or otherwise) that might exist to what the private sector can achieve on its own, against the background of existing rules of the game (supervisory and regulatory frameworks, including financial safety nets). A recent, but by no means unique, example of such a limitation is the private coordination failure that apparently occurred in organizing the private rescue of LTCM. By some accounts, in the days before it became clear that LTCM might default on some of its contracts, several large institutions apparently tried to organize a larger group of institutions to take over the hedge fund. While some were willing to put up substantial amounts of capital, it was in the end insufficient. Moreover, it was also reported that several institu-

---

[103]See Counterparty Risk Management Policy Group (1999) and Basel Committee on Banking Supervision (2000a and 2000b).

tions with financial interests nevertheless decided they would not be a party to such a partnership. This example (of a free-rider problem) represents a limit to the ability of the private sector to ensure the smooth functioning of markets—by coordinating private solutions—in the presence of market stress.

There may also be limits to how far information asymmetries can be reduced. LTCM was widely viewed as a large source of trading revenues and information in 1996 and 1997. Each creditor institution can be viewed as having formulated an investment and trading strategy with LTCM that seemed desirable at the time given the limited information they had. In effect, institutions were involved in a dynamic game with LTCM and within the OTC derivatives markets: they provided financing for LTCM's trades in return for trading activity and a window on LTCM's order flow and investment strategy. Although it is easy, in retrospect, to question why LTCM's counterparts did not demand more information, in a competitive environment, cost considerations must have weighed heavily. Clearly, LTCM's counterparties thought the cost of more information was too high, and walking away from deals was not seen as in their interest. Moreover, they all thought they were receiving useful information from LTCM's orders for trades.

Thus, situations can arise in which institutions in pursuit of self-interest can collectively produce market conditions that become unsustainable and harmful to them individually and collectively. That is, in the absence of a central, coordinating mechanism that enforces collective self-interest in market stability (such as on an exchange), individually desirable strategies, when aggregated, can produce bad market outcomes. Perhaps private information sharing and coordination could have made the LTCM game end without a severe disruption, but so too could have more effective official refereeing. The challenge is to have a framework that is more effective in preventing these situations from arising, and this involves assigning responsibilities to strengthen areas with potential instabilities.

Strengthening Incentives for More Effective Market Discipline

In some cases the assignment of responsibility is obvious. It is clearly the responsibility of private financial institutions to manage individual private risks, within the regulatory and supervisory framework. Well-known improvements (as discussed above and documented in several reports issued since the LTCM crisis) can be made in risk-management and control systems to enhance the likelihood that institutions will remain well capitalized and profitable and thereby help to avoid instability, even in times of stress. The fact that market participants have not moved as quickly as might have been expected to improve risk management systems—given the virulence of the turbulence in the autumn of 1998—suggests that designing and implementing new systems to deal with the complex and evolving risks involved in OTC derivatives is a difficult challenge. On the other hand, while institutions have been slow to move ahead quickly with changes in risk management, there nevertheless is evidence that some of the major institutions are presently devoting less capital to market making in OTC derivatives markets and have also reduced proprietary trading.

Moral hazard, perhaps associated with national histories of market interventions, may be another factor impinging on the effectiveness of market discipline. The risk to financial stability arising from banks' OTC derivatives activities may also be influenced by access to financial safety nets, which by imparting a subsidy element can influence the pricing of risk and thereby lead to overextensions of credit both on- and off-balance-sheet. Access to safety nets (including central bank financing) can give rise to incentives to take additional risks that can lead to the buildup of large, leveraged exposures which, when suddenly unwound, can precipitate a financial crisis of systemic proportions. Moreover, interventions during one stressful episode that limit losses can sow the seeds of the next buildup of exposures. These influences may have dampened the strong potential signal that institutions might have received from the turbulence that followed the near-collapse of LTCM.

It may be time to consider incentives that might be provided by the official sector to encourage the private sector to improve its ability to monitor itself, and to improve the effectiveness of market discipline. As emphasized in International Monetary Fund (1999),[104] one way of improving the ability of private incentives to effectively discipline behavior is for the private and public sectors to jointly identify possible inconsistencies arising from the complex interplay of both private and regulatory incentives as they affect private decisions. Inconsistencies between private and regulatory incentives—for example, inconsistencies between internal models for allocating capital and regulatory capital requirements—could thus be rectified to alter behavior in ways that preserve efficiency and promote market stability.

---

[104]See p. 79 in International Monetary Fund (1999).

Reducing Legal and Regulatory Uncertainty

There also seems to be an obvious assignment of responsibilities in the area of legal and regulatory uncertainty. The official sector and national legislatures can reduce legal and regulatory uncertainty. Legal or regulatory uncertainties that can be clearly identified should be addressed as soon as possible. Three areas immediately come to mind: the regulatory treatment of swaps and the implications for using private clearinghouses; closeout procedures; and netting. In each of these cases, reducing uncertainty could have the adverse consequence of actually increasing risk taking. To ensure that measures to reduce legal and regulatory uncertainty actually strengthen financial stability, it may be desirable, therefore, to link them to measures to address those features of OTC derivatives, institutions, and markets that most clearly pose risks to market stability. For example, legal certainty of closeout and netting would implicitly provide OTC derivatives creditors seniority over general creditors if a counterparty defaults. This could give rise to incentives to engage in riskier activities. To counteract such incentives, the extent of legally sanctioned closeout of contracts and permitted netting of exposures could be made contingent on key structural reforms that enhance stability. In this example, trading arrangements along the lines of a clearinghouse could be treated more favorably with respect to closeout and/or netting. More generally, the public sector should consider how steps to strengthen the legal infrastructure could help promote structural improvements in OTC derivatives markets. With these provisos in mind, the following considerations could potentially reduce the risk of market instability.

First, in the United States, the agencies supervising institutions and regulating markets (including the Federal Reserve System, the Treasury, the SEC, and the CFTC) agree that financial swaps ought to be exempt from CFTC supervision and regulation. The 1999 report by the President's Working Group on Financial Markets on regulation of OTC derivatives recommended removing this uncertainty through legislative reforms that would grant swaps an exemption from potential CFTC oversight.[105] This has been well received by the private sector, and work is underway, but limited progress has been made in this area. Resolving this issue with changes in legislation would clear the way for serious private consideration of reorganizing OTC derivatives markets, including taking advantage of many of the risk-mitigating possibilities of a clearinghouse structure. Although legislation is under consideration in the U.S. Congress, some concerns have been expressed by the Federal Reserve Board, the Treasury, and the SEC about some features of this legislation, and it remains to be seen if the necessary changes will be passed into U.S. law.[106]

If the legal obstacles to a clearinghouse for OTC derivatives are removed, such an arrangement could mitigate risks associated with plain-vanilla swaps by handling clearing and settlement, formalizing and standardizing the management of counterparty risk through margin, and mutualizing the risk of counterparty default, and thereby reinforce market discipline and encourage self-regulation.[107] Another question is whether market participants would need official encouragement to use a private clearinghouse. On the one hand, some market participants have expressed considerable skepticism about such an arrangement, and the clearing arrangements attempted thus far (such as Swap-Clear) have attracted little activity, in part because they are perceived to be costly, including relating to regulatory capital requirements. On the other hand, some market participants see a central clearinghouse as inevitable in view of the considerable operational difficulties of managing an OTC derivatives business, the challenges of managing credit risk on a bilateral basis, and the legal uncertainty of the OTC environment. In any case, if the regulatory environment is liberalized and the legal environment is clarified, this could accelerate the adoption of private electronic trading arrangements for swaps and other OTC derivatives (already in evidence in 2000) and may well give rise to de facto private clearinghouses.

Second, closeout procedures for derivative contracts have proven to be impractical and ineffective in some jurisdictions and under some market circumstances. Had they worked effectively, some of the adverse market dynamics in the LTCM crises might have been avoided. The uncertainty of their applicability might be clarified by the appropriate regulatory and legal bodies, including at the G–10 level if they involve more than one legal jurisdiction. The consequences of inaction could mean that virulent dynamics will not be avoided the next time there are rumors of default in OTC derivatives markets.

---

[105]See United States, President's Working Group on Financial Markets (1999b).

[106]See testimony by Federal Reserve Chairman Greenspan, SEC Chairman Levitt, and Treasury Secretary Summers before the Joint U.S. Senate Committees on Agriculture, Nutrition and Forestry, and Banking, Housing and Urban Affairs on June 21, 2000.

[107]For discussion of issues surrounding clearinghouses, see Hills, Rule, Parkinson and Young (1999), Hills and Rule (1999), pp. 111–12, and Bank of England (2000), pp. 77–78.

Third, netting arrangements are another risk mitigation technique that can help reduce gross creditor and debtor counterparty positions to a single bilateral credit or debit with each counterparty. The uncertainty about the legality and regulatory treatment of these arrangements can give rise to situations of heightened credit risk. Further and stronger efforts should be made to strengthen the legal basis for netting.

Coordinated Improvements in Disclosure

Coordination is particularly necessary in the area of information disclosure. In finance, information is a source of economic rents. There are natural limits to how much of it will be voluntarily provided publicly, or even privately to establish counterparty relationships. Therefore, the private sector is unlikely, on its own accord, to provide the right amount and kind of information to counterparties, the markets, and authorities, unless it has incentives to do so. Accounting standards and prudential rules require certain forms of disclosure. However, there was insufficient information in 1998 for private counterparts, supervisors, or those responsible for market surveillance to reach the judgment that vulnerabilities were growing in the global financial system. The public sector has a strong role to play in providing incentives for greater disclosure to the markets and greater information on a confidential basis to the official sector.

While, in principle, creditors have incentives to demand adequate disclosure from their counterparties, these can be undermined by competitive pressures and concerns by their counterparties that confidentiality might not be protected. To overcome this, emphasis can be placed on strengthening the primacy of credit risk management, including the autonomy of risk management within organizations to make confidentiality credible, in line with proposals by both private and official groups. The public sector role could be limited to assessing and monitoring the quality of risk management and control systems more systematically and thoroughly, including how information is utilized, and also to ensuring that counterparty disclosure is adequate. The counterparty market discipline imposed by creditors could also be strengthened significantly through better pricing and control of the terms of access to credit.

The challenges in improving public disclosure are formidable. The shift in the boundary between private and public information could, by reducing the private information advantage, lessen intermediation activity. The potential consequences for market functioning need to be weighed against the benefits for market participants from more information on risk concentrations. In addition, it will be difficult to guarantee confidentiality, and even more difficult to develop a consensus on what can usefully be disclosed, in what form, to whom, and how often. For these reasons, an eclectic, innovative approach is needed to address these challenges and pitfalls. Supervisors might promote and facilitate more exchange-like OTC market structures, such as clearinghouses and electronic trading and settlement systems, which would support greater transparency and potentially serve as a nexus for information. Supervisors and regulators could facilitate the adoption of such facilities by regulating them lightly and by devising arrangements for multilateral clearing of contracts that are already covered under bilateral master agreements. Addressing this challenge requires close cooperation between public and private sectors to strike the right balance between financial market efficiency and stability.

Private and Public Roles in Reducing Systemic Risk

In the area of systemic risk, it is important that both the private and public sectors work to reduce it. Private market participants can—by developing and implementing effective risk management and control systems and risk-mitigation tools—individually ensure their own viability and soundness even in extreme circumstances. As noted in International Monetary Fund (1999), well-managed and highly capitalized financial institutions are important components of the first lines of defense against systemic financial problems. Improved risk management and control would reduce the potential for excessive risk taking and the buildup of vulnerabilities at individual institutions, and highly capitalized institutions are better able to absorb losses when they occur. If all institutions succeeded in accomplishing these objectives, the effectiveness of the first line of defense against systemic risk—market discipline—would be strengthened. Under the presumption that a chain is only as strong as its weakest link, unless all of the systemically important financial institutions substantially improve their risk management systems, no financial institution can be assured of dealing in OTC derivatives markets with counterparties that are managing their risks well. Thus, there is some—albeit not a strong—incentive for collective private action centered around improving risk management and the financial infrastructure of these systemically important markets. Such collective private action would support the efforts of industry groups such as ISDA, the Group of 30, and more recently the Corrigan and Thieke Group.[108] These efforts should be intensified and accelerated.

In addition to private actions to reduce systemic risk, authorities are responsible for ensuring financial stability, including through prudential regulations, banking supervision, and market surveillance. Regarding prudential regulations, one strong step forward would be for the Basel Committee on Banking Supervision to reconsider capital requirements for off-balance-sheet credit risks. While the Committee's recent proposals go some way toward more effectively recognizing the risks in off-balance-sheet activities, the increasing sophistication of banks in arbitraging capital requirements and the dynamic nature of OTC derivatives exposures is likely to widen existing gaps in the measurement of banks' overall credit exposures, and consequently in setting appropriate capital levels. The Committee should give consideration to ways in which capital charges on OTC derivatives positions could more closely reflect the significant changes (positive and negative) that occur in a bank's current and potential future credit exposures when market prices change. In this context, banks' internal credit risk systems could be required to quantify off-balance-sheet credit exposures (both current and potential) as a basis for appropriate capital charges—subject to verification through effective supervision.

More generally, authorities face the difficult challenge of helping to ensure financial stability without encouraging risk taking beyond some reasonable prudent level, without impeding financial innovations, and without unduly distorting market incentives. In principle, safeguards (including parts of the financial safety net) promote a more desirable equilibrium than would be obtained without them. But the safeguards may also encourage excessive risk taking. The challenge of keeping moral hazard to a bare minimum in the first instance requires the authorities to engage in sufficient monitoring to ensure that the insured institutions and markets take appropriate account of the risks entailed in their activities. This means that banking supervision and market surveillance need to keep abreast of the changing financial landscape and the institutions that change it, and also need to invest in developing analytical frameworks for understanding them.

---

[108]See pages 77–79 and 173–75 of International Monetary Fund (1999).

VIII   Conclusions

Derivatives markets are central to the functioning of global financial markets, and both exchange-traded and over-the-counter derivatives have improved the pricing and allocation of financial risks significantly. OTC derivatives—compared with exchange-traded derivatives—are flexible and innovative. The ability to use them to unbundle financial risk into separate components is an important step in the direction of creating more complete and efficient financial markets. OTC derivatives enable economic agents to define more precisely their risk preferences and tolerances, and more effectively to manage them. These instruments and the markets in which they are traded support the pricing, trading, risk management, and market conditions in all the major bond, equity, and foreign exchange markets. Probably for this reason alone, they are systemically important, but these markets are also comprised of the internationally active financial institutions that intermediate a large share of international capital flows, and also the lion's share of global lending, underwriting, mergers and acquisitions, and trading businesses. In effect, the OTC derivatives markets are composed of a complex network of bilateral, asset-price dependent counterparty exposures that intimately bind the world's largest and most internationally active financial institutions in a very active and fast-paced trading environment at the core of the international financial system.

Modern internationally active financial institutions make significant use of these instruments in part to manage the risks associated with the intermediation and market-making services they provide to clients, but also to manage their own balance sheet risks and to engage in proprietary trading. As Section II explained, in doing so, modern financial institutions are exposed to financial risks that are different, and in some ways more difficult to assess and manage, than in traditional financial intermediation involving on-balance-sheet lending and deposit taking. In effect, the stochastic processes that govern the cashflows associated with OTC derivatives are inherently more difficult to understand, and more unstable during periods of extreme volatility in underlying asset prices. As usual there are tradeoffs, however. Traditional lending and deposit-taking is insulated from some kinds of market risks (but not interest rate risk)—because it records loans at book value—but it runs the risk that the present value of its loan portfolio declines substantially without properly allocating capital to it. Modern institutions, on the other hand, mark positions to market daily for OTC derivatives and thereby have knowledge about their changing risk profiles. But their earning streams are subject to higher recorded volatility and they are subject to more risks associated with market dynamics and liquidity runs in the context of global financial markets.

Unlike the derivatives exchanges, OTC derivatives instruments and markets are essentially unregulated, although they are affected indirectly by national legal systems, regulations, banking supervision, and market surveillance. Nor is the institutional coverage comprehensive, as hedge funds and unregulated securities affiliates are not regulated. Overall, the supervision of financial institutions and market surveillance plays a critical but limited role in ensuring the smooth functioning of OTC derivatives markets, primarily by seeking to ensure the overall soundness of the institutions that comprise them.

Instead an informal framework, relying mostly on market discipline and private voluntary arrangements, ensures smooth market functioning. There are no formal or centralized mechanisms to limit individual or aggregate risk taking, leverage, and credit extension; the pricing and management of the associated risks are decentralized; and each counterpart has its own internal infrastructure for recording, clearing, settling, and managing the contracts over their, at times, long life span. There is no physical or electronic trading platform: instead, the OTC derivatives markets exist on the collective trading floors of the major internationally active financial institutions. Like the strength of a chain composed of separate links, the strength and stability of OTC derivatives markets depends on the strength of counterparties' risk-management and financial soundness. This is why only sophisticated highly credit-rated institutions are a member of the "club" that make up this informal interbank/interdealer market for trading financial risk.

The OTC derivatives framework has worked reasonably well in not impinging dramatically on the soundness of the major institutions that comprise these markets, in part because they have been well capitalized. But it has not worked well in ensuring market stability, and features of contracts, institutions, and the underlying infrastructure are a potential source of risk, not just of instability in segments of OTC derivatives markets, but also to the international financial system. There were episodes of stress, crisis, and turbulence throughout the 1990s, and the risks of instability were most clearly exemplified in the virulent turbulence and dynamics in the most mature financial markets that accompanied the near-collapse of LTCM in the autumn of 1998. The LTCM crisis created such severe price pressures on the major institutions that risk taking and market liquidity diminished to the point where major central banks perceived the risk of a systemic crisis that could have affected real economic activity.

The crisis revealed a number of surprises. First, the reliance on a combination of market discipline and voluntary mechanisms on the one hand, and official oversight on the other hand, failed to prevent a buildup and concentration of counterparty risks and vulnerabilities. Second, some important features of the underlying financial infrastructure—risk management, and reliance on collateral, closeout procedures, and netting arrangements—did not provide the risk reduction and mitigation results that were expected. Third, before, during, and after the turbulence, there was surprisingly little useful information on which to base assessments about the distribution of risks and exposures among the major financial institutions involved in the market. There was also limited information for assessing the systemic potential of the market turbulence. In short, important features of OTC derivatives markets did not perform as expected when they were most necessary: during a very stressful period in which major firms were at risk of suffering losses and many other smaller institutions were at risk of illiquidity if not insolvency.

Section V identified and analyzed key features of OTC derivatives markets that can give rise to the risk of instability. These include: the dynamic nature of gross credit exposures; important information asymmetries; the fact that OTC derivatives activities affect available aggregate credit and market liquidity; that OTC derivatives markets are large and highly concentrated in the global financial institutions; and the fact that OTC derivatives markets are central to the global financial system. There are also several imperfections in the decentralized infrastructure that were revealed during the LTCM crisis, and which have not yet been adequately addressed: inadequate counterparty risk management; the limited understanding of market dynamics and liquidity risk; and legal and regulatory uncertainty. An additional complicating factor is that the major intermediary and market-making institutions have direct access to financial safety nets, and all of them are too big to liquidate rapidly without risking an international financial market disruption. This potentially imparts an element of subsidy in their pricing of counterparty and other risks that can lead to an overextension of credit and market activity.

The combinations of these risks that were evident in the 1990s can all be seen as originating in imperfections in three broad areas—market discipline, risk-mitigating infrastructures, official rule making and oversight. Improvements are essential if the risk of instability is to be reduced in global financial markets.

Unfortunately, it is easier to identify the sources of instability in OTC derivatives markets than it is to find specific remedies, which can only be pragmatically formulated and implemented by private and official practitioners in these markets. Nevertheless, some broad areas are identified in Section VII as deserving particular attention if market disruptions and instabilities of the kind experienced in the autumn of 1998 are to be avoided. In particular, the private sector can reduce the potential for instability through more effective market discipline, risk management, and disclosure. Public efforts are also necessary, particularly to strengthen incentives for market discipline, remove legal and regulatory uncertainties, and improve the effectiveness of OTC derivatives markets surveillance.

In general, while there are good reasons for public sector involvement (existence of safety nets, legal and regulatory uncertainty, and the potential for systemic financial problems with real economic consequences), this does not mean a heavy hand is required, and a case can be made for relying more heavily on *effective* market discipline. The markets are dominated by the internationally active financial institutions, and it is in their individual and collective interest to ensure that financial stability is maintained. To achieve this, the balance of private and official responsibility for preventing problems in OTC derivatives markets, and for resolving them, can and should be shifted more in the direction of market discipline.

In order to rebalance private and official roles, it is essential first to clarify the limits to market discipline in OTC derivatives markets (for example, due to private coordination failures and asymmetric information), before leaning more heavily on aspects of market discipline that seem to work well in these markets. This would require a constructive dialogue between private market participants and those with the responsibility for safeguarding financial stability.

Changes in prudential regulations, and in particular capital adequacy requirements, may be a vital part of this engagement, in part because such changes can further bolster the ability of institutions to withstand the at times strong adverse impact of (shareholder, creditor, and counterparty) market discipline. As noted in the text, even with the 1995 amendment to the 1988 Basel Accord on capital adequacy, there is scope for improving capital adequacy requirements related to credit risks associated with OTC derivatives transactions. The Basel Committee should give serious consideration to ways in which capital charges could more closely reflect the significant changes that occur in a bank's current and potential future credit exposures when market prices change. In that context, banks' internal credit risk systems that quantify off-balance-sheet credit exposures (both current and potential) could serve as a basis for appropriate capital charges—subject to verification through an effective supervisory process.

Second, improvements in counterparty risk management, and risk management more generally, are essential. The 1998 turbulence could not have occurred without the buildup and concentration of risk exposures. This resulted from several sources: financial institutions made mistakes; the risk management systems they relied on were not effective in limiting their exposures; and counterparty, liquidity, operational, and legal risks were not properly assessed, monitored, and managed. Implementation of private initiatives in several areas should be accelerated, especially the recommendations of the Corrigan and Thieke report on counterparty risk management.

Third, the quality of disclosure and information needs to be significantly improved. The scarcity of information and its asymmetry was revealed to be an important aspect of the buildup and the unwinding of positions surrounding the LTCM crisis. It is therefore essential to develop mechanisms to make available the minimum information necessary for effective market discipline and for effective official oversight (supervision and surveillance) in a way that assures confidentiality. Thus, while there are challenges in improving disclosure and transparency without creating disincentives for efficient intermediation, more and useful information is necessary, whether through cooperative and coordinated disclo-

sure by the active institutions, or by mandatory disclosure. Likewise, more, and more effective, private counterparty and market monitoring of OTC derivatives markets is essential. This monitoring can be achieved either by creating incentives for the private sector to provide more information on its own or by making sure in some reasonable way that private market participants are not taking imprudent risks.

Fourth, progress in resolving legal and regulatory uncertainty is achievable. Uncertainties about closeout procedures, netting arrangements, bankruptcy, and recapture of collateral have given, and can still give, rise to severe market dynamics during periods of heightened uncertainty about counterparty risk. The interconnected nature and concentrations of counterparty exposures together with legal and regulatory uncertainty make the OTC derivatives markets especially vulnerable to attempts to rapidly unwind large gross exposures, when in most cases resolving net exposures would suffice. It would be useful to reduce some of this uncertainty, but only if it does not inadvertently lead to even greater risk taking. In return for legal and regulatory certainty, the private institutions that created these markets might have to implement changes to the structure of these decentralized markets and infrastructures in ways that reduce the risks of market instability.

Fifth, as noted in Chapter IV of International Monetary Fund (1999), there also were flaws in the official lines of defense against financial problems (banking supervision and market surveillance). While some progress is being made in specific areas (relating mostly to transparency), banking supervision and market surveillance also need to be adapted to monitor more effectively OTC derivatives activities and markets by, for example, paying closer attention to the impact of OTC derivatives activities on private risks within financial institutions and on private and systemic risks within and across markets.

Collectively, these initiatives can both improve the potential benefits of market discipline and bolster the private sector's ability to avoid and deal with financial problems, and thereby should help reduce systemic risk.

Appendix   Development of OTC Derivatives Markets in Historical Perspective

While derivatives or derivative-like features can be found in the earliest recorded financial contracts, until quite recently derivatives markets, to the extent they existed, were probably relatively illiquid. This Appendix chronicles the development of the preconditions necessary to support the high degree of liquidity that characterizes modern OTC derivatives markets. These include the rise of financial institutions capable of functioning as market makers, the establishment of derivatives exchanges that provide hedging vehicles and enable market makers to manage their risk, and advances in information technology and finance theory that facilitate more accurate pricing of OTC derivatives and measurement of risk.

Derivatives or financial contracts with derivative-like features seem to have existed throughout recorded financial history. Such contracts specify rights or obligations to make or receive transfers depending on the value, or on outcomes affecting the value, of an underlying financial instrument or commodity. They encompass both separate derivatives contracts that can be traded on a market and financial contracts with embedded options or contingent clauses. Derivatives traded on markets differ from other marketable instruments in that their value "derives" entirely from that of an underlying financial instrument or commodity.

Derivative-like features can be found in very early financial contracts. The first recorded example dates back to the time of Hammurabi (1800 BC), ruler of ancient Babylon, and is included in Hammurabi's code, the first formal recorded legal code. The code, which among other things regulated terms of credit, specified that in the event of a crop failure due to storm or drought, interest on that year's land loan would be canceled.[109] This example of a derivative, broadly defined, takes the form of a contingent clause embedded in and modifying a financial contract (the land loan) so as to give it derivative-like characteristics. The clause provides partial insurance against natural disasters by canceling interest payments when they occur.

Financial contracts with embedded options were likely the primary form of derivatives for much of recorded financial history. As financial markets developed, they seem to have evolved into forms resembling existing securities with embedded options. For example, beginning in sixteenth century Europe, convertible securities and preferred stock—instruments with derivative-like properties—appear to have been increasingly used.[110] The main drawback of embedded options was that they could not be traded separately from the underlying instrument.

A key innovation was the creation of derivative instruments that could be traded separately from the underlying financial instrument or commodity. The earliest recorded such instruments appear to have been Venetian government bond forwards in thirteenth century Venice.[111] In this early period, the exchange of financial instruments, and derivatives based on these instruments, seems to have initially taken place on an informal and bilateral basis in locations such as coffeehouses. In the sixteenth century, as financial activity increased in cities like Amsterdam and London, these bilateral contacts evolved into meetings of groups of investors, effectively establishing informal markets for the trading of financial instruments including derivatives. These markets could be regarded as early OTC markets in that they were based on networks of bilateral linkages, although they lacked key institutional features, such as market makers, that are the source of liquidity in modern OTC derivatives markets.

This market activity evidently provided the basis for the creation of exchanges in the emerging financial centers. These early "traditional" exchanges differed significantly from modern exchanges. Rules governing trading were much less restrictive and standardization of contracts was limited. Typically, a wide range of different financial instruments was traded on relatively illiquid markets. The modern distinction between exchange and over-the-counter

---

[109]See Ingersoll (1989).

[110]See Steinherr (1998).
[111]See Chancellor (1999), p. 7.

trading was probably of limited relevance since trading tended to occur on a bilateral basis.

The first organized exchange was founded in Amsterdam in 1610.[112] A wide range of contracts were traded on it, including stocks, commodities, insurance, a form of money market instrument, futures, and stock options. Also, there was a system of margin lending that could be used as a source of leverage.[113] In London, an exchange existed by the end of the seventeenth century, although trading activity seemed to have remained somewhat more decentralized with substantial amounts of trading continuing to occur in other locations such as coffeehouses. For example, trading in equities apparently only became centralized on a single exchange in 1802. Derivatives trading was sharply curtailed in England following the collapse of the South Sea Bubble in the fall of 1720 as the result of legislation banning short sales, which was not repealed until 1836. In the United States, in the late eighteenth and early nineteenth century, the development of securities trading, including derivatives trading, followed the pattern of Amsterdam and London with the founding of the New York Stock Exchange in 1817.

Early derivatives seem to have predominantly been forwards, probably because they were relatively straightforward to value. Equity options were also traded. For example, trading in equity derivatives appears to have become well established in London by the late seventeenth century. Records indicate that these derivatives were used for risk management and speculation. They also show that investors were using relatively sophisticated finance concepts such as present value and discounted cash flow analysis to price them.[114] For example, in 1692, John Houghton, owner of a London coffee shop where equity trading took place, published an explanation of how a put option could be used to hedge against a fall in the price of an equity. During the South Sea Bubble, compensation of South Sea Company management (and bribery of officials) consisted in part of stock options.

While these early derivatives markets resembled modern OTC derivatives markets in that trading occurred through a network of bilateral contacts, they lacked the liquidity of modern OTC derivatives markets, because markets lacked institutions that could act as market makers and provide liquidity by temporarily taking over and holding a seller's derivative positions until a buyer could be located. Market making institutions only developed recently as financial instruments became available to enable them

to hedge and manage the risk associated with this activity and when it became possible to accurately price derivatives and measure their risk. Also, since market making can involve carrying sizable positions, a financial infrastructure to provide the necessary financing needs to be in place. Only with the creation of liquid financial derivatives exchanges did adequate hedging instruments become available. The features of these exchanges were largely derived from modern commodity derivatives exchanges.

The first commodity futures exchange was the Osaka Rice Exchange in eighteenth century Japan. Commodity derivatives exchanges developed in roughly their current form in Chicago in the 1850s. Commodity derivatives exchanges were created to enable agricultural producers and wholesalers to hedge commodity price risk. They differed from the traditional financial exchanges, described above, in that only a limited number of standardized contracts were traded and the terms of contracts and exchange are specified by a relatively detailed set of rules. These features contributed to a high degree of market liquidity, enabling these markets to perform their price discovery function. In time, a regulatory structure developed to strengthen investor protection.

The trading of financial derivatives on modern exchanges—modeled on the commodity derivatives exchange—did not occur until quite recently. The first financial futures exchange was created in Chicago in 1970. In 1973, the first options exchange—trading call options on U.S. equities—opened, also in Chicago and, in 1977, the trading of put options was added. Subsequently, derivatives exchanges opened elsewhere in the United States and other countries such that, by the 1980s, options and futures on hundreds of equities and a wide range of bond, Treasury bill, and foreign exchange contracts were traded. The relatively recent extension of the commodity exchange model to financial derivatives can be partly attributed to several factors: the large number of underlying financial instruments, especially in the case of equities, limited the scope for standardization, making it more difficult to achieve sufficient liquidity; settlement on commodity exchanges was typically in the commodity rather than cash; and commodity exchanges were often located near commodity-producing regions far from the major financial centers where the underlying financial instruments were traded.[115]

The creation of liquid derivatives exchanges in combination with advances in finance theory and information technology provided the preconditions for the development of liquid OTC derivatives based on market makers by allowing them to effectively man-

---

[112]This exchange is still in existence.
[113]See Chancellor (1999), p. 10.
[114]Chancellor (1999), p. 57.

---

[115]Steinherr (1998).

age the risk associated with market making in OTC derivatives markets. Advances in finance theory, notably the Black-Scholes options pricing model, made it possible for the first time to accurately price many types of derivatives. They also facilitated dynamic hedging of derivatives exposures in the markets for the underlying instruments, which was useful in cases where exchange-traded derivatives were not available for hedging. The financial institutions that had been involved in derivatives activity prior to the establishment of these preconditions, either on a bilateral basis or on relatively illiquid traditional exchanges, were well positioned to function as market makers. The fact that in many cases they were large, internationally active financial institutions meant that they typically had access to the financing necessary to perform this function.

The early development of liquid OTC derivative markets was driven partly by incentives for regulatory arbitrage. These arose largely from the need to avoid capital and exchange controls that were essential elements of the post-World War II global financial system. Also, the introduction of capital requirements for banks gave rise to incentives to use OTC derivatives to circumvent or reduce them (by moving exposures off balance sheet). While regulatory arbitrage was important to the creation of these markets, market activity was increasingly driven by hedging and speculation as liquidity improved and the cost of participation fell.

The development of the foreign exchange swap market illustrates the role of regulatory arbitrage in the development of OTC derivatives markets. The first swaps were created in the 1960s to allow U.S. and U.K. multinationals who wanted to borrow in the others' currency to circumvent U.K. exchange controls. Each firm would borrow in its own currency and then swap the principal so that no cross-border transactions were recorded (see Box 3.2: Motives for OTC Derivatives Transactions). The role of financial intermediaries was initially limited to matching counterparties (for example, they func-

tioned as a broker). As swaps became more widely used, intermediaries took on the role of counterparty to each participant, effectively functioning as a market maker. In this capacity, they would carry the foreign currency position of a counterparty until they could find a buyer, who might be another financial intermediary. Their ability to hedge and finance such positions made it possible for them to perform this role.[116]

The development of an extensive and sophisticated OTC market infrastructure in the 1980s and 1990s with many of the world's largest financial institutions serving as market makers has greatly enhanced the liquidity of OTC derivatives markets. This, in turn, has lowered the cost of participation and supported the expansion of the market. Measured by notional principal, OTC derivatives markets have grown to roughly nine times the size of those for exchange-traded derivatives and have approximately the same turnover (see Figure 3.1).

The expansion of OTC derivatives markets will likely continue to be driven by technology and enhancements to the institutional infrastructure. The large volume of trading in some products on OTC derivatives markets has led to an increasing degree of standardization (for example, "plain vanilla" derivatives). The development of electronic trading, and clearing and settlement technologies, is making it possible to increase efficiency by introducing exchange-like trading arrangements for these products. As a result, the distinction between exchange-traded and OTC derivatives may become blurred and OTC products may increasingly compete with and displace comparable products on derivative exchanges.

---

[116]Steinherr (1998). The early development of the swap may be partly due to the fact that foreign exchange exposures are relatively easy for intermediaries to hedge (and need not involve foreign exchange futures). Specifically, intermediaries can hedge foreign exchange exposures by borrowing the currency in which they are long.

Glossary

Book value: The value of an asset that appears on a balance sheet based on historic cost or the original purchase price.

Broker: An intermediary between buyers and sellers who acts in a transaction as an agent, rather than a principal, charges a commission or fee, and—unlike a dealer—does not buy or sell for its own account or make markets. In some jurisdictions, the term "broker" also refers to the specific legal or regulatory status of institutions performing this function.

Choice of law: Provision (for example, in a master agreement) that stipulates the jurisdiction whose law governs an OTC derivatives transaction. The term sometimes is used to refer to the principles by which jurisdiction is determined in a dispute (also known as "conflict of law").

Clearing and settlement: The process of matching parties in a transaction according to the terms of a contract, and the fulfillment of obligations (for example, through the exchange of securities or funds).

Clearinghouse: An entity, typically affiliated with a futures or options exchange, that clears trades through delivery of the commodity or purchase of offsetting futures positions and serves as a central counterparty. It may also hold performance bonds posted by dealers to assure fulfillment of futures and options obligations.

Closeout procedures: Steps taken by a nondefaulting party to terminate a contract prior to its maturity when the other party fails to perform according to the contract's terms.

Collateral: Assets pledged as security to ensure payment or performance of an obligation.

Credit exposure: The present value of the amount receivable or payable on a contract, consisting of the sum of current exposure and potential future exposure.

Creditor stay exemption: The exclusion of certain creditors from the automatic stay provision of the bankruptcy code, which generally limits creditors' capacity to directly collect debts owed by a bankrupt party, including through netting of outstanding contracts. An example is the U.S. Bankruptcy Code statutory exceptions for repurchase agreements, securities contracts, commodity contracts, swap agreements, and forward contracts, where counterparties can close out exempt OTC derivatives positions outside of bankruptcy procedures.

Credit risk: The risk associated with the possibility that a borrower will be unwilling or unable to fulfill its contractual obligations, thereby causing the holder of the claim to suffer a loss.

Dealer: An intermediary that acts as a principal in a transaction, buys (or sells) on its own account, and thus takes positions and risks. It earns profit from bid-ask spreads (and potentially from its positions). A dealer can be distinguished from a broker, who acts only as an agent for customers and charges commission. In some jurisdictions, the term "dealer" also refers to the specific legal or regulatory status of institutions performing this function.

Derivatives (exchange-traded and over-the-counter): Financial contracts whose value derives from underlying securities prices, interest rates, foreign exchange rates, market indexes, or commodity prices. Exchange-traded derivatives are standardized products traded on the floor of an organized exchange and usually require a good faith deposit, or margin, when buying or selling a contract. Over-the-counter derivatives, such as currency swaps and interest rate swaps, are privately negotiated bilateral agreements transacted off organized exchanges.

Fair value: Defined by the Financial Accounting Standards Board as "the amount at which the instrument could be exchanged in a current transaction between willing participants, other than in a forced or liquidation sale."

Forward contract: A contractual obligation between two parties to exchange a particular good or instrument at a set price on a future date. The buyer of the forward agrees to pay the price and take delivery of the good or instrument and is said to be "long the forward," while the seller of the forward agrees to deliver the good or instrument at the agreed price on the agreed date, and is said to be "short the forward." Collateral may be deposited up front, but cash is not exchanged for the good or instrument until the delivery date. Forward contracts, unlike futures, are not traded on organized exchanges.

Futures: A negotiable contract to make or take delivery of a standardized amount of a commodity or securities at a specific date for an agreed price, under terms and conditions established by a regulated futures exchange where trading takes place. It is essentially a standardized forward contract that is traded on an organized exchange and subject to the requirements defined by the exchange.

Haircut: The difference between the amount advanced by a lender and the market value of collateral securing the loan. For example, if a lender makes a loan equal to 90 percent of the value of marketable securities that are provided as collateral, the difference (10 percent) is the haircut. The term also refers to formulas used in the valuation of securities for computing net capital positions of broker-dealers.

Hedging: The process of offsetting an existing risk exposure by taking an opposite position in the same or a similar risk, for example, by purchasing derivatives contracts.

Intermediation: The process of transferring funds from an ultimate source to the ultimate user. A financial institution, such as a bank, intermediates credit when it obtains money from a depositor and relends it to a borrowing customer.

Legal risk: Risk that arises when a counterparty lacks the legal or regulatory authority to engage in a transaction or when the law does not perform as expected. Legal risks also include compliance and regulatory risks, which concern activities that might breach government regulations, such as market manipulation, insider trading, and suitability restrictions.

Leverage: The magnification of the rate of return (positive and negative) on a position or investment beyond the rate obtained by direct investment of own funds in the cash market. It is often measured as the ratio of on- and off-balance-sheet exposures to capital. Leverage can be built up by borrowing (on-balance-sheet leverage, commonly measured by debt-to-equity ratios) or through the use of off-balance-sheet transactions.

Liquidity: The ability to raise cash easily and with minimal delay. Market liquidity is the ability to transact business in necessary volumes without unduly moving market prices. Funding liquidity is the ability of an entity to fund its positions and meet, when due, the cash and collateral demands of counterparties, credit providers, and investors.

Margin: The amount of cash or eligible collateral an investor must deposit with a counterparty or intermediary when conducting a transaction. For example, when buying or selling a futures contract, initial margin must be deposited with a broker or clearinghouse. If the futures price moves adversely, the investor might receive a margin call—that is, a demand for additional funds or collateral (variation margin) to offset position losses in the margin account.

Mark-to-market: The valuation of a position or portfolio by reference to the most recent price at which a financial instrument can be bought or sold in normal volumes. The mark-to-market value might equal the current market value—as opposed to historic accounting or book value—or the present value of expected future cash flows.

Market maker: An intermediary that holds an inventory of financial instruments (or risk positions) and stands ready to execute buy and sell orders on behalf of customers at posted prices or on its own account. The market maker assumes risk by taking possession of the asset or position. In organized exchanges, market makers are licensed by a regulating body or by the exchange itself.

Market risk: The risk that arises from possible changes in the prices of financial assets and liabilities; it is typically measured by price volatility.

Master agreement: Comprehensive documentation of standard contractual terms and conditions that covers a range of OTC derivatives transactions between two counterparties.

Moral hazard: Actions of economic agents that are to their own benefits but to the detriment of others and arise when incomplete information or incomplete contracts prevent the full assignment of damages (and/or benefits) to the agent responsible. For example, under asymmetric information, borrowers may have incentives to engage in riskier activities that may be to their advantage, but which harm the lender by increasing the risk of default.

Netting arrangement: A written contract to combine offsetting obligations between two or more parties to reduce them to a single net payment or receipt for each party. For example, two banks owing each other $10 million and $12 million, respectively, might agree to value their mutual obligation at $2 million (the net difference between $10 million and $12 million) for accounting purposes. Netting can be done bilaterally—when two parties settle contracts at net value—as is standard practice under a master agreement, or multilaterally through a clearinghouse. Closeout netting combines offsetting credit exposures between two parties when a contract is terminated.

Notional amount/principal: The reference value (which is typically not exchanged) on which the cash flows of a derivatives contract are based. For example, the notional principal underlying a swap transaction is used to compute swap payments in an interest rate swap or currency swap.

Off-balance-sheet items: Financial commitments that do not involve booking assets or liabilities, and thus do not appear on the balance sheet.

Operational risk: Risk of losses resulting from management failure, faulty internal controls, fraud, or human error. It includes execution risk, which encompasses situations where trades fail to be executed, or more generally, any problem in back-office operations.

Option: A contract granting the right, and not the obligation, to purchase or sell an asset during a specified period at an agreed-upon price (the exercise price or strike price). A call option is a contract that gives the holder the right to buy from the option seller an asset at a specified price; a put option is a contract that gives the holder the right to sell an asset at a predetermined price. Options are traded both on exchanges and over-the-counter.

Over-the-counter (OTC) market: A market for securities where trading is not conducted on an organized exchange but through bilateral negotiations. Often these markets are intermediated by brokers and/or dealers. Examples of OTC derivatives transactions include foreign exchange forward contracts, currency swaps, and interest rate swaps.

Performance bonds: Bonds that provide specific monetary payments if a counterparty fails to fulfill a contract, thereby providing protection against loss in the event the terms of a contract are violated.

Potential future exposure (PFE): The amount potentially at risk over the term of a derivatives contract if a counterparty defaults. It varies over time in response to the perceived risk of asset price movements that can affect the value of the exposure.

Replacement value/cost: The current exposure adjusted to reflect the cost of replacing a defaulted contract.

Swap: A derivatives contract that involves a series of exchanges of payments. Examples are agreements to exchange interest payments in a fixed-rate obligation for interest payments in a floating-rate obligation (an interest rate swap), or one currency for another (a foreign exchange swap). A cross-currency interest rate swap is the exchange of a fixed-rate obligation in one currency for a floating-rate obligation in another currency.

Value at Risk (VaR): A statistical estimate of the potential marked-to-market loss to a trading position or portfolio from an adverse market move over a given time horizon. VaR reflects a selected confidence level; therefore, actual losses during a period are not expected to exceed the estimate more than a prespecified number of times.

References

Bank for International Settlements, 2000, *The Global OTC Derivatives Market Continues to Grow* (Basel).

Bank of England, 2000, *Financial Stability Review*, Issue No. 8 (June).

Basel Committee on Banking Supervision, 1995, *Basel Capital Accord: Treatment of Potential Exposure for Off-Balance-Sheet Items* (Basel: Bank for International Settlements).

———, 2000a, *Banks' Interactions with Highly Leveraged Institutions: Implementation of the Basel Committee's Sound Practices Paper* (Basel: Bank for International Settlements).

———, 2000b, *Sound Practices for Managing Liquidity in Banking Organisations* (Basel: Bank for International Settlements).

Basel Committee on Banking Supervision and Technical Committee of the International Organization of Securities Commissions (IOSCO), 1999, *Trading and Derivatives Exposures of Banks and Securities Firms* (Basel).

Breuer, Peter, 2000, "Measuring Off-Balance-Sheet Leverage," forthcoming IMF Working Paper (Washington: International Monetary Fund).

Bryant, John, 1980, "A Model of Reserves, Bank Runs, and Deposit Insurance," *Journal of Banking and Finance*, Vol. 4 (December), pp. 335–44.

Cass, Dwight, 2000, "Master Master," *Risk*, Vol. 13 (March), p. 16.

Caxton Corporation, Kingdon Capital Management, LLC, Moore Capital Management, Inc., Soros Fund Management, LLC, Tudor Investment Corporation, Sullivan & Cromwell, and Rutter Associates, 2000, *Sound Practices for Hedge Fund Managers* (New York: Rutter Associates).

Chancellor, Edward, 1999, *Devil Take the Hindmost: A History of Financial Speculation* (New York: Farrar, Straus and Giroux).

Clow, Robert, 2000, "Swapping Identities," *Institutional Investor* (International Edition), Vol. 25 (February), pp. 121–25.

"Collateral Calculations," 1999, *Futures and OTC World*, Issue No. 343 (December), pp. 44–47.

Counterparty Risk Management Policy Group, 1999, *Improving Counterparty Risk Management Practices* (New York).

Covitz, Daniel M., Diana Hancock, and Myron L. Kwast, 2000, "Mandatory Subordinated Debt: Would Banks Face More Market Discipline?" working paper, Board of Governors of the Federal Reserve System, June.

Diamond, Douglas W., 1984, "Financial Intermediation and Delegated Monitoring," *Review on Economic Studies,* Vol. 51 (July), pp. 393–414.

Diamond, Douglas W., and Philip H. Dybvig, 1983, "Bank Runs, Deposit Insurance, and Liquidity," *Journal of Political Economy*, Vol. 91 (June), pp. 401–19.

Dunbar, Nicholas, 1999, "Sterling Swaptions: Volatility by the Pound," *Risk*, Vol. 12 (September), pp. 23–28.

Folkerts-Landau, David, and Alfred Steinherr, 1994, "The Wild Beast of Derivatives: To Be Chained Up, Fenced In or Tamed?" in *The AMEX Bank Review Prize Essays: Finance and the International Economy*, Vol. 8 (New York: Oxford University Press for American Express Bank).

Global Derivatives Study Group, 1993, *Derivatives: Practices and Principles: Appendix I: Working Papers* (Washington: Group of Thirty).

Grabbe, J. Orlin, 1991, *International Financial Markets* (New York: Elsevier, 2d. ed.).

Greenspan, Alan, 1998, "Risk Management in the Global Financial System," remarks at the Annual Financial Markets Conference of the Federal Reserve Bank of Atlanta, Miami Beach, Florida, February 27.

———, 2000, "Over-the-Counter Derivatives," testimony before the U.S. Senate Committee on Agriculture, Nutrition and Forestry, February 10.

Group of Thirty, 1993, *Derivatives: Practices and Principles* (Washington).

———, 1997, *Global Institutions, National Supervision and Systemic Risk: A Study Group Report* (Washington).

Hills, Bob, and David Rule, 1999, "Counterparty Credit Risk in Wholesale Payment and Settlement Systems," *Financial Stability Review*, Bank of England, Issue No. 7 (November), pp. 98–114.

———, Sarah Parkinson, and Chris Young, 1999, "Central Counterparty Clearing Houses and Financial Stability," *Financial Stability Review*, Bank of England, Issue No. 6 (June), pp. 122–34.

Hull, John C., 2000, *Options, Futures, & Other Derivatives* (Upper Saddle River, New Jersey: Prentice-Hall, 4th ed.).

Ingersoll, Jonathan E., 1989, "Option Pricing Theory" in *The New Palgrave: Finance*, ed. by John Eatwell, Murry Milgate, and Peter Newman (New York: W. W. Norton).

International Monetary Fund, 1996, *International Capital Markets: Developments, Prospects, and Key Policy Issues,* World Economic and Financial Surveys (Washington).

———, 1998a, *International Capital Markets: Developments, Prospects, and Key Policy Issues,* World Economic and Financial Surveys (Washington).

———, 1998b, *World Economic Outlook and International Capital Markets: Interim Assessment*, World Economic and Financial Surveys (Washington).

———, 1999, *International Capital Markets: Developments, Prospects, and Key Policy Issues,* World Economic and Financial Surveys (Washington).

International Swaps and Derivatives Association, 1999, *ISDA 1999 Collateral Review* (London).

———, 2000, *Collateral Arrangements in the European Financial Markets, The Need for National Law Reform* (London).

Kawaller, Ira, 1999, "Toward an International Accounting Standard: Is Fair Value a Fair Measure?" *Middle Office*, Issue No. 5 (Winter), pp. 31–37.

Kindleberger, Charles P., 1989, *Manias, Panics, and Crashes: A History of Financial Crises* (New York: Basic Books).

Kolb, Robert W., 1996, *Financial Derivatives* (Cambridge: Blackwell, 2d. ed.).

Kroszner, Randall S., 1999, "Can the Financial Markets Privately Regulate Risk? The Development of Derivatives Clearinghouses and Recent Over-the-Counter Innovations," *Journal of Money, Credit and Banking,* Vol. 31 (August, Part 2), pp. 596–623.

Lau, Frederic, 1997, *Derivatives in Plain Words* (Hong Kong: Hong Kong Monetary Authority).

Lyons, Richard K, 1996, "Foreign Exchange Volume: Sound and Fury Signifying Nothing?", in *The Microstructure of Foreign Exchange Markets*, ed. by Jeffrey A. Frankel, Giampaolo Galli, and Alberto Giovannini (Chicago: University of Chicago Press).

Mahtani, Arun, 1999, "Credit Investment Enters New Era," *International Financing Review,* Issue No. 1306 (October 23), p. 90.

Malz, Allan, M., 1995, "Currency Option Markets and Exchange Rates: A Case Study of the U.S. Dollar in March 1995," *Current Issues in Economics and Finance*, Federal Reserve Bank of New York, Vol. 1 (July).

Marshall, John F., and Kenneth R. Kapner, 1993, *Understanding Swaps* (New York: Wiley & Sons).

Rainer, William J., 2000, Testimony by CFTC Chairman Rainer before the U.S. Senate Committee on Agriculture, Nutrition and Forestry, February 10.

Remolona, Eli M., William Bassett, and In Sun Geoum, 1996, "Risk Management by Structured Derivative Product Companies," *Federal Reserve Bank of New York Economic Policy Review*, Vol. 2 (April), pp. 17–37.

Schinasi, Garry J., and R. Todd Smith, 1999, "Portfolio Diversification, Leverage, and Financial Contagion," IMF Working Paper 99/136 (Washington: International Monetary Fund).

Smith, Claire, 2000, "Credit Derivatives: Fastest-Growing Risk Protector," *Financial Times Survey: International Capital Markets, Financial Times,* May 19.

Smithson, Charles, and Gregory Hayt, 1999, "Credit Derivatives Go From Strength to Strength," *Risk*, Vol. 12 (December), pp. 54–55.

Staehle, Daniel C., and Christina M. Cumming, 1998, "The Supervision of Credit Derivatives Activities of Banking Organizations," in *Handbook of Credit Derivatives*, ed. by Jack Clark Francis, Joyce A. Frost, and J. Gregg Whittaker (New York: McGraw-Hill).

Steinherr, Alfred, 1998, *Derivatives: The Wild Beast of Finance* (New York: Wiley & Sons).

Summers, Lawrence H., 2000, Testimony by U.S. Treasury Secretary Summers before the U.S. Senate Committee on Agriculture, Nutrition and Forestry, February 10.

Thom, Jamie, and Louise Boustani, 1998, "The Foreign Exchange and Over-the-Counter Derivatives Markets in the United Kingdom," Bank of England *Quarterly Bulletin*, Vol. 38 (November), pp. 347–60.

Tietmeyer, Hans, 1999, Remarks at the conference of the Center for Financial Studies on Systemic Risk and Lender of Last Resort, Frankfurt, June 11–12.

Trant, Henry, 1999, "Settling Up," *Futures and OTC World*, Issue No. 342 (November), pp. 65–67.

United Kingdom, Financial Services Authority, 1999a, *The London Code of Conduct: For Principals and Broking Firms in the Wholesale Markets* (London).

———, 1999b, *The Regulation of the Wholesale Cash and OTC Derivatives Markets Under Section 43 of the Financial Services Act 1986* (London).

United States, Board of Governors of the Federal Reserve System, 1997, *Supervision and Regulation Letter 97–18*, June 13.

———, 1999, "International Activities of U.S. Banks and in U.S. Banking Markets," *Federal Reserve Bulletin,* Vol. 85 (September), pp. 599–615.

———, 1999, "Using Subordinated Debt as an Instrument of Market Discipline," Staff Studies No. 172 (Washington).

United States, Commodity Futures Trading Commission, 1993a, *Study of Swaps and Off-Exchange Derivatives Trading* (Washington).

———, 1993b, *The Report of the Commodity Futures Trading Commission: OTC Derivatives Markets and Their Regulation* (Washington).

———, 1999, *Regulation of Over-the-Counter Derivatives Transactions* (Washington).

United States, Commodity Futures Trading Commission Staff Task Force, 2000, *A New Regulatory Framework* (Washington).

United States, General Accounting Office, 1999, *Long-Term Capital Management: Regulators Need to Focus Greater Attention on Systemic Risk* (Washington).

United States, Office of the Comptroller of the Currency, 2000, *OCC Bank Derivatives Report, Second Quarter 2000* (Washington).

United States, President's Working Group on Financial Markets, 1999a, *Hedge Funds, Leverage, and the Lessons of Long-Term Capital Management* (Washington).

———, 1999b, *Over-the-Counter Derivatives Markets and the Commodity Exchange Act* (Washington).

United States, Securities and Exchange Commission, 1997, *Net Capital Rule* (Washington).

———, 1999, *Final Rule: OTC Derivatives Dealers* (Washington).

Wallace, Ian, 1994, "Legal and Documentation Issues of Swaps and Financial Derivatives," Part 44 in *Swaps and Financial Derivatives*, by Satyajit Das (Sydney: The Law Book Company, 2d. ed.)

White, Andrew, 1997, "Credit Exposure in OTC Derivatives: A Risk Management Challenge," *Financial Stability Review*, Bank of England, Issue No. 2 (Spring) pp. 60–67.

Recent Occasional Papers of the International Monetary Fund

180. Revenue Implications of Trade Liberalization, by Liam Ebrill, Janet Stotsky, and Reint Gropp. 1999.

179. Disinflation in Transition: 1993–97, by Carlo Cottarelli and Peter Doyle. 1999.

178. IMF-Supported Programs in Indonesia, Korea, and Thailand: A Preliminary Assessment, by Timothy Lane, Atish Ghosh, Javier Hamann, Steven Phillips, Marianne Schulze-Ghattas, and Tsidi Tsikata. 1999.

177. Perspectives on Regional Unemployment in Europe, by Paolo Mauro, Eswar Prasad, and Antonio Spilimbergo. 1999.

176. Back to the Future: Postwar Reconstruction and Stabilization in Lebanon, edited by Sena Eken and Thomas Helbling. 1999.

175. Macroeconomic Developments in the Baltics, Russia, and Other Countries of the Former Soviet Union, 1992–97, by Luis M. Valdivieso. 1998.

174. Impact of EMU on Selected Non–European Union Countries, by R. Feldman, K. Nashashibi, R. Nord, P. Allum, D. Desruelle, K. Enders, R. Kahn, and H. Temprano-Arroyo. 1998.

173. The Baltic Countries: From Economic Stabilization to EU Accession, by Julian Berengaut, Augusto Lopez-Claros, Françoise Le Gall, Dennis Jones, Richard Stern, Ann-Margret Westin, Effie Psalida, Pietro Garibaldi. 1998.

172. Capital Account Liberalization: Theoretical and Practical Aspects, by a staff team led by Barry Eichengreen and Michael Mussa, with Giovanni Dell'Ariccia, Enrica Detragiache, Gian Maria Milesi-Ferretti, and Andrew Tweedie. 1998.

171. Monetary Policy in Dollarized Economies, by Tomás Baliño, Adam Bennett, and Eduardo Borensztein. 1998.

170. The West African Economic and Monetary Union: Recent Developments and Policy Issues, by a staff team led by Ernesto Hernández-Catá and comprising Christian A. François, Paul Masson, Pascal Bouvier, Patrick Peroz, Dominique Desruelle, and Athanasios Vamvakidis. 1998.

169. Financial Sector Development in Sub-Saharan African Countries, by Hassanali Mehran, Piero Ugolini, Jean Phillipe Briffaux, George Iden, Tonny Lybek, Stephen Swaray, and Peter Hayward. 1998.

168. Exit Strategies: Policy Options for Countries Seeking Greater Exchange Rate Flexibility, by a staff team led by Barry Eichengreen and Paul Masson with Hugh Bredenkamp, Barry Johnston, Javier Hamann, Esteban Jadresic, and Inci Ötker. 1998.

167. Exchange Rate Assessment: Extensions of the Macroeconomic Balance Approach, edited by Peter Isard and Hamid Faruqee. 1998

166. Hedge Funds and Financial Market Dynamics, by a staff team led by Barry Eichengreen and Donald Mathieson with Bankim Chadha, Anne Jansen, Laura Kodres, and Sunil Sharma. 1998.

165. Algeria: Stabilization and Transition to the Market, by Karim Nashashibi, Patricia Alonso-Gamo, Stefania Bazzoni, Alain Féler, Nicole Laframboise, and Sebastian Paris Horvitz. 1998.

164. MULTIMOD Mark III: The Core Dynamic and Steady-State Model, by Douglas Laxton, Peter Isard, Hamid Faruqee, Eswar Prasad, and Bart Turtelboom. 1998.

163. Egypt: Beyond Stabilization, Toward a Dynamic Market Economy, by a staff team led by Howard Handy. 1998.

162. Fiscal Policy Rules, by George Kopits and Steven Symansky. 1998.

161. The Nordic Banking Crises: Pitfalls in Financial Liberalization? by Burkhard Drees and Ceyla Pazarbaşıoğlu. 1998.

160. Fiscal Reform in Low-Income Countries: Experience Under IMF-Supported Programs, by a staff team led by George T. Abed and comprising Liam Ebrill, Sanjeev Gupta, Benedict Clements, Ronald McMorran, Anthony Pellechio, Jerald Schiff, and Marijn Verhoeven. 1998.

159. Hungary: Economic Policies for Sustainable Growth, Carlo Cottarelli, Thomas Krueger, Reza Moghadam, Perry Perone, Edgardo Ruggiero, and Rachel van Elkan. 1998.

158. Transparency in Government Operations, by George Kopits and Jon Craig. 1998.

Note: For information on the title and availability of Occasional Papers not listed, please consult the IMF Publications Catalog or contact IMF Publication Services.